# How to be a Little SOD

# Simon Brett

# How to be a Little SOD

illustrated by
## Tony Ross

VICTOR GOLLANCZ

LONDON

## TO
## VIRGINIA AND BILL,
### who are a bit closer to it

First published in Great Britain September 1992
Second impression October 1992
Third impression November 1992
Fourth impression November 1992
Fifth impression December 1992
Sixth impression December 1992
Seventh impression November 1993
Eighth impression August 1994
Published by Victor Gollancz
A Division of the Cassell group
Villiers House, 41/47 Strand, London WC2N 5JE

A catalogue record for this book is
available from the British Library

ISBN 0 575 04160 9

Photoset in Great Britain by
Rowland Phototypesetting Ltd, Bury St Edmunds, Suffolk
and printed in Great Britain by
St Edmundsbury Press Ltd, Bury St Edmunds, Suffolk

# First Month

## DAY 1

Well, here I am. After the nine months I've just been through, this had better be good!

I'd decided while all the pushing was going on to be very brave about the whole business. But when I actually emerged, all I got for my bravery was panic-stricken faces, shouts of 'The baby's not crying!' and the immediate indignity of being up-ended and slapped on the bum.

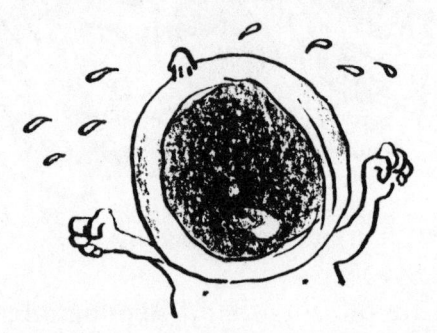

So I gave them what they wanted and let out an enormous bellow. That went down much better.

The bum-slapping was hardly over before it was replaced by another indignity: an obsessive interest in my private parts. I suppose they had been waiting for nearly nine months to find out what sex I was, but they could have been slightly more restrained.

Next thing, I'm bundled up into a blanket and thrust into Her arms. 'Oh, isn't oo beautiful then?' She starts cooing. 'Isn't oo wonderful then?'

It was, through all the schmaltz, an interesting moment – my first chance to see the face of the woman who'd been my mobile home for the past nine months.

I have to say She wasn't looking Her best. And was all that crying *really* necessary?

Not that She was the only one. Over Her shoulder I could see the other half of the conspiracy – Him. He was in an even worse state – pale, trembly and, again, tears pouring down the cheeks.

Clearly they go in for crying in a big way out here. So I joined in, loudly.

But there's no pleasing them. A minute before, they were all desperate because I *wasn't* crying: suddenly now I'm getting all this 'There's no need to cry, come on, baby, don't cry, there's a lovely baby . . . '

What *do* they want?

The rest of my first day was *so* undignified: they cut off my lifeline with Her. They washed me, weighed me and clothed me in a horrible, shapeless all-in-one outfit. By the end of it, though, I had realised one important truth – viz. my parents are totally dependent on me, and respond instantly to my slightest change of mood.

In fact, a significant ground rule has already been established: I'M THE ONE IN CHARGE.

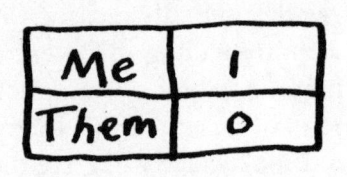

# DAY 2

This morning Her parents came to visit me. Apparently I look exactly like She did as a baby.

They brought me a present – a rattle shaped like a teddy bear's head on a stick. 'I'm sure baby'll soon be playing with that,' they said. Huh – the day you catch me playing with decapitated teddy bears . . .

Her parents asked about names for me. I can only hope my parents' suggestions were demonstrations of a lively sense of humour.

Her parents asked when the christening was going to be. My parents ummed and erred a bit.

Really got stuck into this feeding business. She's very nervous about it. She's always known theoretically that that's what Her breasts were designed for, but it's not something that can be tested out on a dry run.

Already She's worried about not producing enough milk for me. Good point to remember: WITHHOLD-ING MY AGREEMENT TO EAT WILL BE A USEFUL FORM OF EMOTIONAL BLACK-MAIL.

When He came to visit, He brought the camera. She

had washed Her hair, put on a bit of makeup and a clean nightdress to look as good as currently possible (not very) for the official photographs.

Thought I'd managed to mess things up nicely by puking over Her clean nightdress just as He pressed the button, but He seemed actually pleased to have got a shot of that. I have a funny feeling my every action over the next few weeks is going to be seen as a photo opportunity.

In the afternoon His parents came to give me the once-over. Apparently I look exactly like He did as a baby.

They brought me a present – a rattle shaped like a teddy bear's head on a stick. 'You're sure baby hasn't got one like that?' they asked. 'Oh no,' She replied.

Why did She lie? I detect potential family conflict here – a bit of tension between the rival grandparents.

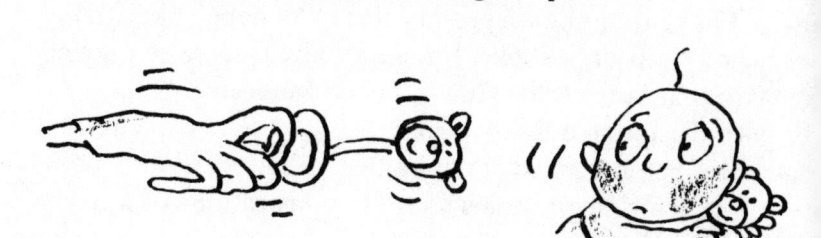

His parents asked about names. My parents' suggestions just cannot be serious.

His parents also asked about the christening.

Later on, She had a bit of an argument with the ward sister. She's convinced of the value of demand feeding, while sister thinks it won't do me any harm to wait four hours between feeds.

Sister is of course right, but I'm glad to say She is being allowed to follow Her system. This is good news for me, because demand feeding offers much more potential for disruption and general mayhem.

Sister still disapproves and mutters darkly that She is 'making a rod for Her own back'. Too right She is.

## DAY 3

A big day. I am taken home from hospital.

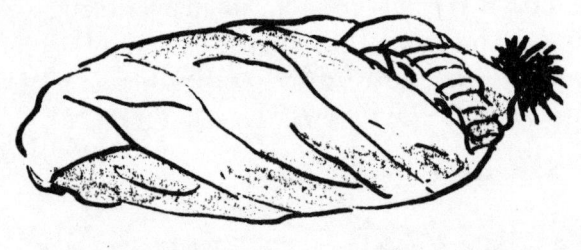

They wrapped me up so well, I could hardly see through my eye slits. Even so, couldn't help being a little disappointed in the house. You don't have a lot to think about during that nine months' wallow in the womb, and I'm afraid I did nurse the odd fantasy about being born into the monied classes.

Even briefly entertained the notion of the Royal Family . . .

Still, what can you do?

As soon as we got there, I was whisked upstairs to my nursery with lots of 'Oo's got a super room then?' and 'Isn't iss a uvvy nursey for oo then?' (I really wish they'd cool it with the 'thens'.)

9

I would have liked to agree about the nursery, but I'm sorry . . . My parents may have many admirable qualities, but taste – well, forget it.

For instance, there, hanging over the cot – directly in the eye-line of anyone tucked into it – is a mobile of fluffy crocodiles. Really! Any child who grows up thinking that crocodiles are cuddly is going to get a nasty surprise in later life! The WWF has got a lot to answer for.

Already I long for the day when I can stand up in my cot, grab hold of the nearest fluffy crocodile and PULL THE WHOLE BLOODY THING DOWN!

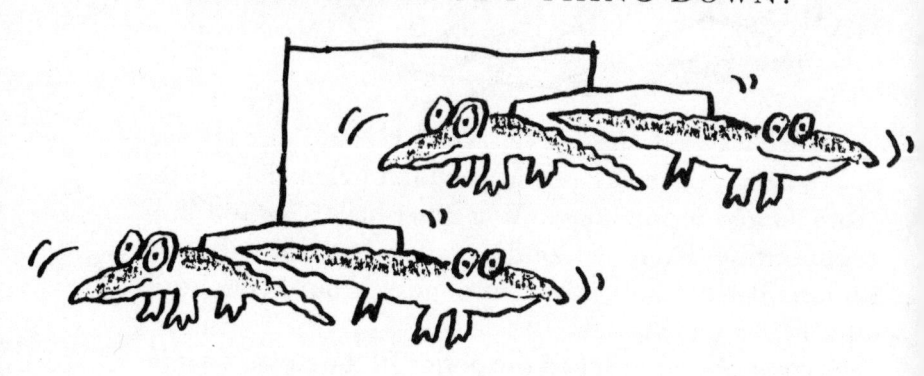

## DAYS 4–5

These two days have been taken up by visitors coming to pay homage to me, starting with His godmother. Apparently I look exactly like His Uncle Wilfrid while he could still recognise people.

She brought me a present – a bib with Ninja Mutant Turtles on it. I ask you. You can tell she got that on the cheap – nothing dates as quickly as yesterday's spin-off merchandising.

And yes, the godmother asked when the christening was going to be.

# DAY 6

Visited by Her friend from work. Apparently I look exactly like Princess Michael of Kent. Ergh.

The friend brought me a present – a bib with Mickey and Minnie Mouse on it. At least that wasn't bought on the cheap, but I do resent becoming a party to the Disney Consumerworld so early in my life.

# DAY 7

Visited by His colleague from the office. Apparently I look exactly like the milkman-her-her-her.

He brought me a present – a packet of condoms. 'Both sexes carry them nowadays,' he said. 'Never too early to be prepared-her-her-her.' This had clearly seemed an amazingly good joke after a few drinks with friends at lunchtime. She seemed markedly less amused by it than he did.

The colleague didn't mention anything about a christening, but did say that he was going out with Him tonight for a few jars to wet the Baby's head-her-her-her.

I noticed the milk was a bit sour at my next feed.

## DAY 9

Today I met my potential enemy.

The cat. Clearly acquired as a surrogate object for their affections before they went all the way and had me.

It was hatred at first sight. The cat spat at me, so I cried.

Of course I'll win in the long run. At the moment, though, the cat has the advantage of me. It is extremely mobile, and I am extremely immobile. But I'm working on it.

## DAY 10

I've discovered another potential hazard of life. She has a book on childcare.

I know I'm going to see a lot of that book over the next few months. My every tiny development will be monitored and checked against the relevant entry.

Mind you, it means all I have to do, if I want to get Her really twitchy, is to come up with something that's not covered in the index.

## DAY 11

Because She was totally knackered by my continuous demand feeding, He announced magnanimously that He would take charge of me for the evening while She had a 'well-earned' rest.

But it was pathetic. He's even more nervous than She is. Consulted that book every two minutes like He was trying to defuse a bomb by correspondence course.

Only lasted three-quarters of an hour. Then, in a state of total paranoia, He went rushing upstairs to wake Her, convinced that I was suffering from every ailment listed in the index.

The only thing he managed to do during that three-quarters of an hour was change my nappy. Well, sort of.

But was He proud of himself?

'It can't be the nappy,' He announced, as they both ran down to match my (non-existent) symptoms to the list of ghastly childhood illnesses. 'I changed the nappy.'

That line's going to be heard a good few times in the next months. I can just see Him, in the pub at lunchtime with his mates, grinning modestly and saying, 'I do my bit, you know. Obviously, my wife spends more time with the baby, because I'm at work all day, but I help out when I get home. I mean, for example . . . I change the baby's nappies.'

Real New Man, He is. My Dad.

# DAY 12

Great excitement today. I went out in my pram for the

first time. Very bumpy over the front step – I hope She puts in a bit of practice with an empty pram before our next excursion.

Only went for a short trip: up the road, and along a row of shops to the chemist.

Then we went back home, mission unaccomplished. You see, the only reason for taking me out had been to show me off to friends and acquaintances and She didn't meet anyone. There was even a girl She'd never seen before serving in the chemist.

## DAY 13

Another excursion in the pram. She still hasn't mastered the front step.

This morning was a bit better on the social front, although She had to go up and down the road three times before She met anyone She knew.

Those She did meet seemed impressed with me – I should think so too.

Three thought I looked exactly like Her, two thought I looked exactly like Him and one thought I looked exactly like Winston Churchill. Huh.

One asked about names. She said the decision had finally been made. Then She told them.

They have *got* to be joking.

## DAY 14

Out in the pram again. Fractionally better in getting me over the doorstep, but She still needs practice.

Went to the clinic. Got weighed, etc. Drew admiring glances from other mums – only to be expected, really. She met a neighbour also there with a baby (hideous little beast, in my opinion). As the neighbour loomed over me to get a good look, I put on my best looking-exactly-like-Her face.

'Ooh,' said the neighbour. 'Doesn't baby look like Daddy . . . ?'

I don't know why I bother.

## DAY 15

Very satisfactory confrontation with the cat today.

It came into my nursery mid-afternoon when I was supposed to be having a sleep. I didn't immediately start crying. No, I let the poor creature do its usual preliminary kneading of the bedspread before settling down on the divan. I even allowed it to start purring.

Then I tried out a new trick I've been practising for a while. It's a wild arm-flailing routine whose flying finger-nails nearly always guarantee a scratch on my cheek.

The moment I'd achieved a nice little nick I started bawling. Instantly She's in the nursery. One look at my face and She jumped to exactly the conclusion I'd intended.

The cat was swept up and slapped mercilessly.

Minute it was released, it shot downstairs and out through the cat-flap. Hasn't been seen since.

## DAY 20

Today I learnt a new word. Actually, She's only just learnt it too. Up till now She hasn't known how to describe my habit of depositing little dollops of puke on Her shoulder whenever She lifts me up.

But She's been at the book again and now She knows that the word for this phenomenon is a 'possetting', and the deposit itself is known as a 'posset'.

Now I know the proper term for it, I'm determined to improve the timing and accuracy of my 'possetting'.

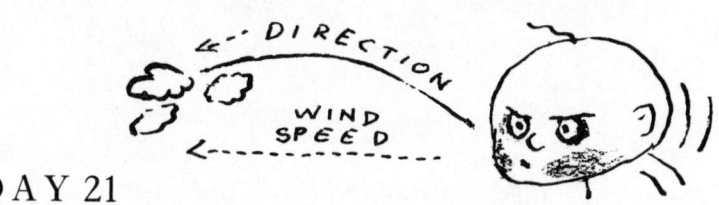

## DAY 21

A day largely given over to possetting practice.

The trick is not to throw up while actually being lifted and in the mother's eye-line but to hold it in until you've been placed neatly over Her shoulder.

Then you've got to be subtle. Full-scale vomiting, even at that angle, is easily spotted. The true possetter's skill lies in allowing a little glob of puke to slip imperceptibly out of the mouth, so that She is unaware of the white deposit on the back of Her navy-blue jumper until She catches sight of it when passing a mirror, or wonders in Sainsbury's why She feels like She's been followed round all day by a lump of mouldy cheese.

## DAY 22

Spent the day polishing up my possetting. Slowly working my way through Her wardrobe. Another trip in the pram. To the dry cleaner's.

## DAY 23

Still making good progress on the possetting front (or, to be strictly accurate, the possetting back). Haven't managed to soil any of Her best clothes yet, but give me time. The health visitor came today to look me over. Apparently I still have the right number of limbs.

## DAY 26

She has taken to putting a muslin nappy over Her shoulder each time She picks me up. Frustrating. I suppose I've got the health visitor to thank for that.

# DAY 28

She had an invitation to coffee today. For tomorrow morning. Clearly, from what She said to Him about Her hostess, it's someone She wants to impress with how-little-She-has-let-my-arrival-change-her-way-of-life.

If She believes that . . .

# DAY 29

The coffee morning was one of my biggest triumphs so far. Her hostess was a career feminist, determined that she herself would never 'end up tied to the house by a baby'.

Once we'd arrived, She did Her best: a lot of nonchalant swinging me around as if I'd been one of Her accessories for years, and the full 'Oh, I've been determined from the start that the baby'll have to fit in with *my* schedule' routine.

I bided my time till the moment when my efforts would have maximum impact.

It came after about forty minutes. Her nonchalance now veering on the casual, She swung me up over Her shoulder.

With pin-point accuracy, I produced the perfect posset. Not only did it enslime the back of Her black linen jacket, it also dripped glutinously down on to the hostess's expensively upholstered sofa.

Within five minutes we were on our way back home.

And Her jacket had to go to the dry cleaner's.

Am I good or am I *good*?

# Second Month

## DAY 1

I am not sure that His intentions towards Her are entirely honourable.

Thinking I'd dozed off during my feed in their bed this evening, He tried to move me out of the way and get closer to Her.

I was rather put out. After all, She is my Mum.

## DAY 2

He had another go this evening.

To give Her Her due, She didn't encourage Him. In fact, She pushed Him away and asked tetchily if He ever thought about anything else.

He said He did sometimes think about other things but it had been months and months, hadn't it, for God's sake?

She replied that the doctor had said they must wait. Till after Her six-week check-up. 'Which is only another ten days, after all.'

The way He stomped off towards the sitting room and the whisky bottle suggested He reckoned ten days was a lot longer than She did.

## DAY 7

Experimented with a new kind of crying. It's more piercing, and I do a bit of shaking and sobbing between yells.

It worked a treat. Brought that paranoid look into Her eyes.

Then I pretended I was hungry, but lost interest in the nipple as soon as it was offered, and started crying again. The new crying, of course.

She went straight to that book.

By the time He'd got back from the office, She'd found what She was looking for in the index: 'Three-month colic'.

I like that. Very posh. Nice to have an official-sounding medical explanation for the fact that I'm just being a little sod.

And it gives me complete licence to behave absolutely appallingly for the next few weeks.


## DAY 10

I don't like the way things are going. I overheard Her being very affectionate to Him in their bedroom this evening.

I soon put a stop to that by breaking into my new kind of crying.

I indulged in my three-month colic all night, not allowing a consecutive ten minutes to go by without bawling.

If I can't actually stop them from touching each other, I can at least see to it that they're too tired to enjoy the experience.

## DAY 11

Continued doing everything in my power to exhaust them.

## DAY 12

It was Her six-week check-up today, back at the hospital. And She had the cheek not to take me with Her. Left me with Her mother, to add insult to injury. But at least it gave me the chance to catch up on my sleep, so I'll be ready for them tonight.

She came back at lunchtime looking radiant (or at least as radiant as someone wearing a nursing bra can look), and announced that She had a clean bill of health.

Her mother said she was delighted to hear this, adding slyly that she could think of one person who'd be even more delighted to hear it. How vulgar! Still, at least the reminder gave me time to plan my campaign.

Didn't start the real heavy-duty screaming till the moment He got in from the office. Thereafter I ensured that one or other of them was up with me all night. Don't think they were alone together long enough to take advantage of her clean bill of health . . .

## DAY 13

. . . unless they managed a quick encounter between 3.14 and 3.17, when I did doze off briefly.

But if they did, they must've been too tired to enjoy it.

## DAY 15

Saturday. Her parents came to pay homage. They still thought I looked exactly like She did as a baby. They also brought me another present – a dangly thing to hang from the side of my cot. If you pull on the ring at the bottom – as they insisted on demonstrating far more times than was necessary – it plays 'Raindrops Keep Falling On My Head'. I don't think I'll bother.

They also asked if a date for the christening had been decided. My parents said it wasn't quite confirmed yet.

The longer it stays unconfirmed the better, so far as I'm concerned. The thought of that dreadful name they've given me getting the blessing of the church is quite appalling.

# DAY 16

Sunday. His parents came to pay homage. They still thought I looked exactly like He did as a baby. They also brought me another present – and yes, you've guessed – it was a dangly thing to hang from the side of my cot. If you pull on the ring at the bottom it plays 'Raindrops Keep Falling On My Head'. Couldn't they at least have found one with a different tune?

And when His parents asked, 'You're sure baby hasn't got one like that?' She replied, 'Oh no.'

They also asked about the christening.

I've noticed that my parents don't invite both sets of grandparents over at the same time.

# DAY 17

I don't like it. I think She's getting used to having me around. I heard Her talking on the telephone this morning when She thought I was asleep.

'Oh, we'd love to come to dinner,' She trilled. 'No, the baby won't be any problem. Sleeps through the evenings now. We'll just bring along the Moses basket, put it in a bedroom or whatever, and forget about it till we want to go home.'

Then She had the bottle to say, 'We're not going to let the fact that we've got a baby change the way we run our social life.'

Well! Talk about throwing down the gauntlet.

## DAY 18

Had been toying with the idea of doing my first smile around now but, after what She said on the phone about this dinner party, they can whistle for it.

## DAY 22

Nearly slipped up and inadvertently let out a smile after my feed this morning. Just in time, managed to convert it into a belch.

## DAY 23

She's been at the book again and discovered that a baby should produce its first smile some time between a month and six weeks. They're both now worried sick that I haven't done it.

Trouble is, their anxiety is so comical that I'm having a lot of difficulty in stopping my lips from twitching.

# DAY 25

This was the evening of the dinner party, and I may modestly state that the occasion was an indisputable triumph.

For me, that is.

They'd really done themselves up for the occasion. She was wearing a new dress, which He'd bought Her 'as a reward for getting your figure back so quickly after the baby.'

(Actually, I'm rather miffed by the speed with which She's slimmed down since my arrival. Still, I can comfort myself with the thought that Her hips will probably always be broader, and as for the stretch marks . . . well, those are for life, aren't they?)

I pretended to go to sleep in the car, and they tried to smuggle me in through their friends' hall with the light turned off.

But just as their friends were hovering over me whispering ecstatically about how beautiful I was, I decided to do a full waking-up routine. I felt Her tense up but defused the situation by letting out a winsome little gurgle, before sighing, putting my thumb in and apparently going back to sleep.

'Aah, what a delightful little baby,' they all agreed.

She installed me in a spare bedroom, and left me with a whispered, 'Now oo let Mummy and Daddy have a nice grown-up evening and oo's Mummy'll give oo a nice feed when oo gets home then?'

I kept quiet, waiting for a moment that would cause maximum disruption. I could hear that they were having drinks.

Then my cue came. Movement from downstairs, relaxed voices fluting upwards as they moved into the dining room. I counted to ten and then let rip.

Instantly She was upstairs, with me out of the Moses basket and into Her arms.

I could have played the three-month colic card, but decided to keep that in reserve.

Instead, I did my grunt-and-strain routine. That has to be the nappy, doesn't it?

So She whisked me into the bathroom, unpopped my Babygro and efficiently slipped off the nappy, reacting with some surprise to the fact that it wasn't even wet.

Timing is one of the most important skills in life, and I must say I was really pleased with the way I timed the next bit. A very quick grunt-and-strain was rewarded by direct hits not only on the Babygro and the bathroom carpet, but also on her new dress.

How's that for marksmanship? Just wait till I get on to solids!

Well, that set the pattern for the rest of the evening. I bawled each time I was put down, I screamed each time I was picked up. I did a perfect impression of a baby in the terminal stages of three-month colic. And I managed to devastate another three nappies, along with any soft furnishings that came within range.

My parents lasted till quarter to ten, then gathered up all my gear and beat a mortified retreat.

'The baby won't be any trouble' – Huh, it'll be a while before they dare use that line again!

# DAY 26

Ever magnanimous in victory, today I gave my first smile.

She looked so miserable after last night's trouncing that I couldn't resist it.

I waited till the evening when He was home from the office. He was in a bad mood. The night before had really brought home to Him how much my arrival was going to change their social life. As a result, He wasn't very nice to me, or to Her.

So She was a little weepy when She put me down in my

cot, and it was then that I decided to cheer Her up with that first smile.

She couldn't believe it straight off. Just picked me up with a mumbled 'Has oo got wind then?'

I smiled again. Nothing.

To speed up Her painfully slow perception, I added a cheery gurgle to the contortion of the lips and, finally, the penny dropped. 'Baby's smiling!' She cried at the top of Her voice. 'Baby's smiling!'

It had the desired effect. He came hurtling up the stairs, and peered soppily into my cot.

Instantly I started screaming.

He's going to have to earn *His* first smile.

## DAY 27

Still only smiling at Her, not at Him. She is very chuffed about this. He is very miffed.

I'm getting the hang of this emotional blackmail business. Think I could have hours of harmless fun in the future, playing one of them off against the other.

## DAY 28

Damn. I overslept, and there is absolutely no doubt that

they used that extra, unmonitored half-hour to get up to something. Can't think of any other explanation for His fatuous grin and the silly sniggers they exchanged when I was finally brought into their bed.

I made them pay for it, don't worry. Screamed inconsolably, wouldn't settle to my feed and, when I finally did, sucked so hard that She's now extremely sore.

Sorry, but this is getting territorial. It's the kind of thing that has to be sharply nipped in the bud (a fairly accurate image, I imagine, for the way She feels, having just fed me).

# *Third Month*

## DAY 2

Overheard Her on the phone boasting to a friend about
what a beautiful baby I am, much more beautiful than
other babies because I have lots of hair. I don't object to
this kind of thing in principle – it is, after all, true – but
don't like the way *She* keeps taking all the credit for it.

Then She said She'd even been considering entering me
for a Beautiful Baby Competition. Hm.

Started moving my head from side to side against the
sheet in my cot.

## DAY 3

Continued rubbing
head on sheet.

## DAY 4

Overheard Her talking to Him about the Beautiful Baby
Competition, which is being held at the end of the month.
They both seem quite keen on the idea. Needless to say,
I'm not.

Also worried by the fact that He has started taking

*artistic* photographs of me. He is no longer content with any picture that isn't taken from a funny angle or through ferns. He'll be entering those for competitions next.

Increased the vigour of my head-rubbing.

## DAY 5

Head-rubbing starting to pay off. She noticed a distinct bald patch when She fed me this morning.

## DAY 7

Almost all the hair has gone from the left side of my head. Look as if I've got mange.

## DAY 8

Now concentrating on the right side of my head. The hair is coming out in handfuls, much to Her distress.

For good measure, am also developing a mild case of cradle cap.

## DAY 10

I am now completely bald, and my scalp is encrusted with

scales. At the clinic today, I drew pitying glances from the other mums. She was covered with embarrassment.

No further talk of entering me for the Beautiful Baby Competition.


# DAY 12

Christening's reared its ugly head again. Overheard Her talking to Her mother on the telephone about it.

She said that, if it was up to Her, of course She'd have me christened, but He had very strong feelings about it and thought it was hypocritical to have a child christened unless you went along with every detail of the Christian faith.


# DAY 13

Overheard Him talking to His mother on the telephone.

He said that, if it was up to Him, of course He'd have me christened, but She had very strong feelings about it and thought it was hypocritical to have a child christened unless you went along with every detail of the Christian faith.


# DAY 14

Overheard them having a blazing row about whether or not they were going to get me christened. He said that, since neither of them went to church, to do it would be hypocritical. A principle was a principle, after all.

Huh.

# DAY 15

Overheard Him on the telephone again this evening. Talking to His mother; it was obvious from the way He was squirming. He finished the conversation by saying it'd be difficult, but He'd see what He could do.

Then I heard Him talking to Her, saying that He hated to see Her unhappy and so, if She really insisted, He would compromise His principles – out of love for Her – and let me be christened.

Oooh, He's devious.

Then She rushed to the telephone to tell Her mother that She had managed to win Him round, and the christening would be on Sunday week.

Later, when He knew She was safely glued to the television, He rang His mother back. He told her He'd managed to win Her round, and the christening would be on Sunday week.

Then, as an afterthought, He rang the vicar. From His end of the conversation, it was apparent that:

A) the vicar was up to here with christenings for at least six weeks, and
B) he only christened the babies of people who attended his church regularly.

# DAY 17

They bought a new piece of baby equipment today. It's a sling.

They both tried me on in it this evening. I prefer being strapped to Her front than His. Well, wouldn't you?

Actually, the sling is extremely comfortable, but I wasn't going to let them know that, so I did the full kicking and screaming routine each time they tried to put me into it.

# DAY 20

She took me to the shops in the sling. Quite enjoyable.

Infuriating when I'm hungry, though. Having my face jammed into Her breasts and being kept away from having a quick feed by a couple of layers of fabric and a nursing bra is one of the most frustrating experiences I have yet encountered.

Mind you, it does open up a whole new territory for possetting.

## DAY 21

She thinks the sling is wonderful, and carried me around in it for most of the day.

In the evening She retired to Her bed with a bad back.

## DAY 22

Saturday. She fed me in bed. Still can't get up because of Her bad back.

## DAY 23

Sunday. A new experience for me. They took me to church.

And, from the way they kept standing up when everyone else sat down and vice versa, it seemed to be a new experience for them too.

At the end of the service, as everyone was filing out, He introduced Himself to the vicar. 'I talked to you about the christening . . . ' He said. 'You remember, you said it'd be all right if we were regular churchgoers . . . ?'

'That's right,' the vicar agreed. 'But I wouldn't call coming once *regular*, would you?'

## DAY 24

'Do you think baby's eyes are all right?' She asked Him

anxiously, as the pair of them hovered over my cot at bedtime tonight. 'I mean, you don't think baby's got a squint, do you?'

Honestly, what *do* they want? If I don't look at them when they put me to bed, they get all hurt and go on about me not caring, and if I do look at them they start worrying that I've got a squint.

Huh. You try looking up from the depths of a cot at two people three times your height *without* squinting.

## DAY 25

Practising my squint. Since they seem determined to worry about it, the least I can do is to give them something visible to worry about.

## DAY 26

Doing rather well with the squint-work. Find if I really concentrate and stare fixedly at the end of my nose with both eyes, the results are excellent (i.e. She gets very worried).

She was so worried that She asked the next-door neighbour in to get her views on the squint. I scuppered that little plan by pretending to be asleep until the neighbour left.

## DAY 27

I'm getting really good at this. Actually got Her standing over my cot with that book in Her hands. It's always a sign that She's seriously worried, when She gets out the workshop manual and starts comparing me with the illustrations.

In fact, when a double-glazing salesman called She even asked him in to give his opinion as to whether I had a squint or not. He said he wasn't sure. She only got rid of him after two hours by ordering a patio door.

## DAY 28

They say that practice makes perfect so spent all the time I was awake with my eyes focused on the end of my nose.

Today it was a Jehovah's Witness She asked in to check out my squint. He said he wasn't sure either, then stayed for three hours and only agreed to leave in exchange for Her soul – and mine too.

## DAY 29

She's *really* worried about it now. Overheard Her reading to Him from the section on squinting in that book: apparently very young babies are expected to squint, but if they go on doing it after a couple of months it means they've actually got A SQUINT. With each day that passes, She becomes more convinced that I've got one.

## DAY 30

They took me to church again. This time I screamed throughout the service. The vicar said it was nice to see them again, and maybe in a couple of weeks they could all have a talk about the possibility of my being christened.

She asked him whether, as an objective outsider, he thought I had a squint or not. The vicar said he wasn't sure, but that God cared equally for all mankind, even the squinters. This didn't seem to reassure Her much.

In fact, by this evening anxiety had reached such a pitch that She phoned the doctor. She considered that it was an emergency and wanted him to come round straight away. The doctor was of the view that, with squints, not a lot's going to change in twenty-four hours, and that this was a Sunday, for God's sake! He said he'd come tomorrow.

She hovered anxiously over my cot just before She went to bed. I opened my eyes, and tried a new variation – looking at the little birds on the right-hand side of my cot with my left eye and those on the left-hand side of my cot with my right eye.

It worked a treat. She burst into tears, and He, who'd had other – less high-minded – plans for the evening, had to be solicitous and comforting well into the small hours.

## DAY 31

Doctor came. I kept my eyes dead straight. He couldn't see anything wrong with them.

Doctor went. As soon as She came upstairs to look at me, I focused my right eye on the left-hand little birds and the left one on the right-hand little birds.

She did not react at all.

Hm. Can it be that She's beginning to see through my tiny ruse?

# Fourth Month

## DAY 1

Today, without warning, She started me on solids.

At the end of my lunchtime feed I was about to have a little zizz, when suddenly I felt this piece of plastic shoved into my mouth. It was a spoon.

She's been at the book again. I bet it says in there that 'you should start your baby on solids after three months'. She takes everything so literally that that's exactly what She's done. To the day.

And the annoying thing is that to some extent She's succeeded. Taking advantage of the surprise factor, She did actually manage to get some of the muck inside me. While the spoon was in my mouth, I did a kind of reverse burp of complaint and inadvertently swallowed the contents.

Yuk. It was a dirty trick.

## DAY 2

Her dirty trick was countered by a much dirtier trick when she had to deal with my first post-solids nappy.

## DAY 3

I'm still making an enormous fuss about this solids business, but I do find myself a bit torn. I have to admit that I quite enjoy them. Not the taste – they don't taste of anything much – but the texture. Once you've had the experience of something with a bit of body down the digestive tract, milk does feel a bit insipid.

Still, I won't let Her know that. Don't want to give Her the impression that She's winning.

| Me | 1 |
|-----|-----|
| Her | ½ |

## DAY 4

I'm only just beginning to realise the potential of this solid food business. Dribbling, possetting and nappy-filling with milk obviously bring great satisfaction, but that's nothing compared to what you can do with solids!

Already my parents' clothes, carpets, furniture, wallpaper, car and even the cat (when I'm lucky) bear witness to my move away from the breast. The possibilities for further chaos are limitless.

Also my hair's started growing again. That gets nicely gunged up with solid food too.

# DAY 6

Sunday again, and that meant another visit to church. I really think they are getting a taste for it. Their movements were much more in unison with the rest of the congregation than they have been the last two weeks, and they even got a couple of the responses in the right places.

And it seems that, so far as the vicar's concerned, three consecutive attendances at church qualifies as 'regular'. Shaking hands with my parents after the service, he conceded that I could be christened in three weeks' time.

I don't like the sound of it one bit.

And when His parents came to see me later, I got another nasty shock.

After lunch, His mother suddenly produced a poncy lace dress out of her bag and announced, 'This is the family christening dress, which you were christened in, darling, and your father was christened in, and your grandfather and great-grandfather were christened in.

You will be using this on the big day, won't you, darling?'

As if I'd allow myself to be seen dead in a garment like that.

# DAY 8

Today I came across one of the disadvantages of going on to solids. A new bib.

Not a towelling one, like I'm used to, though. This number's made of rigid plastic, with a sort of gutter at the bottom, presumably to catch all the gunk I dribble down.

Of course, I screamed the minute she tried to put it on me, but She persevered, and eventually got the thing round my neck, locking some kind of clasp at the back.

She took no notice of my redoubled screams, and began to feed me. I reacted by spitting every spoonful out, then started a head-swivelling and bib-grabbing routine trying to get the thing round to the back of my neck.

It didn't work! The bib got sort of jammed in front, and all my strenuous efforts did was to make me feel as if I was being decapitated.

I've a nasty feeling She may be going to win this one.

# DAY 13

Sunday. We didn't go to church today.

I think that could be good news. If they cease to be regular in their attendance, maybe the vicar will withdraw his consent and the christening will be off.

Later on, Her parents came to see me (my parents're still, very sensibly, keeping the two sets of grandparents apart). After lunch, Her mother suddenly produced a poncy lace dress out of her bag and announced, 'This is the family christening dress, which you were christened in,' etc., etc.

She assured them that I'd be wearing it at my christening.

Looking at it close to, I saw that it was even poncier than the other one.

I think I'm going to have to do a growth spurt over the next two weeks, so that I don't fit into either of them.

## DAY 14

Something else that has been building up for a few weeks has now come to a head. Literally. Even though until recently I hadn't got any hair, She still insisted on washing it in the bath every night. As a result, hair-washing time became tantrum time.

And now I have got hair again, I see absolutely no reason to discontinue my appalling bathtime behaviour.

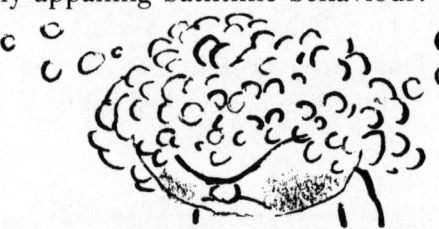

## DAY 16

She is up to something. I was gearing myself up at bathtime for the big fight over hair-washing – quite looking forward to the usual screaming match, watching Her getting more and more frazzled – when suddenly She let me down. Washed all the other bits, didn't touch my hair.

She's been reading Her book again. I bet it's got a section on child psychology.

## DAY 17

She did the same thing in the bath tonight – acted like I didn't have any hair. What *is* She playing at?

I'll wait and see what She tries next. If She lays off the hair completely, I may be reduced to making a fuss about some other bit of me being washed . . .

Genitals, I think . . . She's already slightly nervous about washing that area. If I scream every time She puts Her hand near, it should really give Her a complex.

## DAY 18

Tried the genital screaming trick at bathtime and can report modest success. A look of paranoia came into Her eyes and She rushed off to consult that book.

I bet it's got a section on sexual guilt.


## DAY 19

Have been working hard on my growth spurt.

The date of the christening is looming.


## DAY 20

Sunday, and we didn't go to church this week either. Unfortunately, the vicar rang after lunch and the christening is definitely going ahead.


## DAY 21

Really concentrated on my growth spurt. Ate lots of solids.

# DAY 23

More work on the growth spurt. Solids coming out of ears (as well as the more traditional places).

# DAY 24

Heard my parents arguing this evening about which christening dress I was going to wear on Sunday. He said His one had been in the family for centuries. She said it looked as if it had, and at least the people who'd bought Hers in the first place had had some taste . . .

Vicious stuff. I kept out of it and concentrated on spurting.

# DAY 25

As soon as He had gone to the office this morning, She got out Her family christening dress and tried it on me.

She couldn't fit me into it (with a bit of help from me!).

She was desolate, and wept for most of the day.

When He got home, he left Her sobbing and came upstairs. He got out His family christening dress and tried it on me.

He couldn't fit me into it!

Yippee! My growth spurt has worked.

# DAY 26

Parents!

They went out to the shops this morning and bought me a christening dress even poncier than the other two!

# DAY 27

My christening.

My abiding feeling is one of shame, the shame that can only be felt by someone in a poncy dress who's been splashed liberally with water by someone else in a poncy dress.

I would make a full report of the whole grisly event, but words fail me . . .

I never knew my parents had so many relations! I am totally exhausted by the effort of looking like each one of them in turn.

Only one thing about the whole business interests me – how old do you have to be before you can change your name by deed poll?

# Fifth Month

## DAY 5

I have to admit, She is rather sweet. She really tries hard
to make my life interesting. Trouble is, since She hasn't a
clue what things feel like from my point of view, She rarely
succeeds.

For instance, look at the food She gives me. Not what I
get from Her breasts, I'm referring to the solids.

Some of these, mostly the cereals, She mixes from
packets. The others come in little glass jars, with their
combination of ingredients marked on the label. Egg and
Potato . . . Liver and Cabbage . . . Bacon and Prune . . .
that kind of stuff.

What's touching is the way She refers to these as if I
have strong opinions about them.

'Now shall oo have some lovely Ham and Pea then?' She
asks as She spoons a dollop of beige sludge into my mouth.

'Now doesn't oo like oo's Orange and Blackcurrant
then?' She asks as I turn my head away from another
dollop.

'Oo, yummy-yummy, it's oo's favourite – scrummy Lamb and Greens dinner, isn't it then?' She coos as another little jar is broached.

What She fails to understand is that all these mixtures TASTE EXACTLY THE SAME. It doesn't matter what's on the label – could be Gammon and Pineapple, Venison and Game Chips or Rollmop and Brie – they all taste like soggy cardboard.

The cereals are no different: indeed, with those I wonder why they bother to separate the contents from the packaging.

# DAY 9

'I'm getting a bit worried about the baby's Socially Inter-active Skills,' I heard Her saying this evening.

Oh-oh. When She talks like that, it can only mean one thing. She's been at the book again.

'Oh, really?' He replied. 'I would have thought they were fine.'

The subtext is obvious. What He's really saying is, 'Oh, for God's sake! Can't you stop going on about the baby for a single minute? I've been working hard all day. All I want is a quiet drink and maybe a bit of uncomplicated sex later. I certainly don't want a discussion about our child's "Socially Interactive Skills".'

What it turns out She's talking about, through all the jargon, is my relationships with other people, people in the world outside, people I don't know, even – heaven forbid – other babies.

That book has been nothing but trouble from the day She first opened it. What's got Her aerated this time is some fatuous theory about babies who spend time with other babies from an early age becoming better socially adjusted human beings in later life, going on to form strong bonding relationships and enduring marriages, and no doubt ending up as captains of industry, Justices of the Peace and recipients of MBEs and Nobel prizes.

Oh God.

They didn't pursue the subject this evening. He managed to deflect it by switching the television on.

But I know Her. She won't let it go. Once She gets an idea into Her head, it's there to stay.


# DAY 11

Nothing yet on the SIS front.


# DAY 13

Still nothing. But I won't be lulled into a false sense of

security. It's just when She thinks my guard is down that She's most likely to make a move.

## DAY 14

I was right. Whisking me out of the house this morning with lots of unnerving 'Oo's going to have a uvvy day today then?' kind of chat, She drove me off in a direction we hadn't taken before.

And yes, She took me into a house that contained half a dozen other babies.

Immediately I expressed my dim view of the situation by screaming my head off and soiling a nappy. Trouble is She's getting used to these tactics, and just changed me automatically.

I continued bawling when placed on the floor amidst the other babies.

God, they were a dull lot – seemed incapable of doing anything except screaming their heads off and soiling their nappies.

But I quickly noticed something significant: there were considerably fewer mothers in the room than there were babies. Very suspicious. It only took the word 'super-

52

market' to make me realise exactly what their devilish little plan was.

These mothers were actually trying to get TIME TO THEMSELVES. They didn't give a damn about Socially Interactive Skills. They were simply abandoning their offspring while they went gallivanting off to the fleshpots of Sainsbury's.

Well, some of the other babies may have fallen for such a blatant con trick, but not me. The minute She moved towards the door, I let out a redoubled bellow.

Her step hardly faltered, so I resorted to a new trick I've been working on in private. If I scream and scream *without taking any breaths*, my face very quickly turns purple.

Worked a treat. She scooped me up off the floor and tried to calm my frenzy, but there was no way I was going to stop till She admitted defeat and took me home.

Some of the other mothers gathered round, offering their feeble suggestions as to what might be wrong with me. The general consensus seemed to be that I was suffering from wind.

I was quite happy with this. Not very original, but wind and three-month colic seem to have worked as excuses for everything over the last four months, so why change a winning formula?

One of the mothers, though, did offer an intriguing alternative. Because I kept clutching at my mouth (hamming up my distress as much as possible), she suggested that maybe I was teething. It was about time, she reckoned.

I hadn't thought of this before, but I like the idea. Offers even more possibilities than wind.

For a start, with teething the scale's less restricted. A baby supposedly suffering from wind is picked up, soothed and patted until, given the way the internal system works, up comes a belch, signalling the end of the crisis and a return to the cot.

But a baby picked up supposedly suffering from teething's got a lot more options. The only possible resolution to that crisis is the appearance of a tooth, and that can take a long time.

Yes, no question about it, from now on I'm going to give up wind and do teething.

It certainly did the business this morning. Ten minutes of the purple face and teething routine, and She surrendered ignominiously and took me home.

## DAY 15

I thought She would have got the message and given up on the SIS idea after yesterday's failure, but no, She actually had the nerve to try it on again this morning.

Needless to say, the minute I was put down with the other babies I gave Her the full works, purple cheeks and all, but She actually managed to stick it out for twenty minutes before taking me home.

Her threshold of resistance is rising. This is a worrying development.

## DAY 16

She's very stubborn. She took me to that house *again* this morning. And, once we were there, She demonstrated a shocking new side to Her character.

She left me! Just like that! Plonked me on the floor amidst all those other, common little babies, and, ignoring my full teething extravaganza, calmly announced, 'I'm going to Sainsbury's. The screaming will stop the minute I'm out of the door.'

I made sure She was wrong about that at least. I screamed solidly till the moment She returned, and continued as She hastily grabbed me and made for home. I also managed to posset all over one of the other mothers, and dirty the jumper of yet another who rashly undertook to change my nappy.

But I am still in a state of shock about Her callousness. She can't be allowed to get away with it.

# DAY 19

She's done it again – dumped me with all those other babies, and gone off on her own!

To add insult to injury, She wasn't even going to Sainsbury's. (I'm not unreasonable, I understand that She has to go there from time to time to stock up on jars of soggy cardboard, nappies and other necessaries.) But this morning, She had the brazen effrontery to go and get Her hair cut!

Having Her hair cut doesn't do anything for me. In fact, it brings me a very positive disadvantage, because there's less of the stuff for me to pull and smear with congealed solids.

I must change my tactics.

# DAY 20

She's getting so uncaring. This morning She took me to the crèche and walked off without even a backward glance. Then, when She returned and heard the full extent of my distress during Her absence, She dismissed it with, 'Oh, just playing up. Soon grow out of it'.

Well, She may have been right on the first, but I'll see to it She's wrong about the second!

# DAY 23

Tried a new approach this morning. Marooned in the middle of the other babies as usual, I made no sound of complaint at all. Not a whimper. She reckoned this indicated I was indeed 'growing out of it'.

Poor deluded woman.

I waited till one of the other babies, who could move around a bit better than most of us, crawled across to take a close look at me. He thrust his dozy face into mine, no doubt developing the kind of Socially Interactive Skills that will see him rise in later life to the top of some council's Town Planning Department.

I hung on till the perfect moment, then lashed out with my right hand. My tiny nails left a satisfying weal down his cheek and he burst out screaming. Instantly he got scooped up by his distraught mother, whose attitude to Her when She got back from the Body Shop (more feckless self-indulgence) was distinctly frosty.

I'm getting there.

# DAYS 24–25

The weekend. Spent it tormenting the cat and studying its methods of retaliation. Fortunately it's still too scared of Her actually to touch me, but it did demonstrate some very nifty paw and claw work.

# DAY 27

Dumped among the other babies yet again, I put my study of the cat to good use.

SCORE: 4 babies and 2 mothers with scratched faces.
OUTCOME: Total victory. On Her return from another self-indulgent foray (this time to Benetton, for God's sake!), She was politely asked if She would mind not bringing me to the crèche again. I was thought to be a disruptive influence.

Great! I've developed all the SIS I want.

Notice with interest the subject was not mentioned when He came back from work this evening.

# Sixth Month

## DAY 3

Since the doomed SIS experiment, I've been using teething as an excuse for everything they used to put down to wind.

So imagine my shock this morning when I was woken up by an authentic pain in my gums! This is it – I am actually teething. And, so far, I don't much care for it.

To add to my annoyance, I overheard Her saying to Her mother on the phone this morning, 'Oh yes, baby's still teething.'

'*Still* teething!' I wanted to scream. 'I've only just started!'

Then She went on, 'I'd better get used to it, though. According to my childcare book, babies produce twenty teeth in their first two and a half years.'

Twenty! Two and a half years! Good God, I haven't even got one yet! If they all hurt as much as this, I'll have gone potty before I'm two and a half!

At least I'll see to it I don't suffer alone.

# DAY 4

Spent most of the night screaming, drooling and scrabbling at my mouth with my fingers. Made sure that neither of them got much sleep.

As soon as the shops were open, She rushed round to the chemist and bought some gel stuff to rub on my gums and a bottle of pink, sticky liquid which was supposed to help me sleep. She was advised to use it 'only if the baby's really very distressed. Just the one teaspoonful at that age – and it's very dangerous to exceed the stated dose!'

She rubbed some of the gel on my gums the minute we got home. Useless! It took the pain away for about a minute, if that. Tasted nice, though.

And thereafter it was diminishing returns. The midnight application only took the pain away for a nanosecond.

# DAY 5

By half past two, She was desperate. Out came the bottle of sleeping draught. I made a great fuss, but she probably managed to get half the recommended one teaspoonful down me.

And it worked. I slept through till half past eight.

Then of course I recommenced screaming, drooling and scrabbling at my mouth with my fingers.

So She tried something new that had been recommended by a friend She meets at the clinic – teething rusks. She got a box of those little finger-shaped ones on ribbons and pinned one to my front. I ignored it and just screamed on.

She kept putting the rusk to my mouth to show me the idea, but I wasn't having any.

When He came home, He had a go. Being all jolly and Good-Fatherish, He picked up one of the rusks and said, 'Look – lovely teething rusk. Yum, yum.' Then, to show me what to do, He took a great big bite at it. Broke a tooth.

He suddenly became very much less jolly and Good-Fatherish.

She didn't want to go straight to the sleeping draught this evening, but He insisted. Apparently He'd fallen asleep at His desk this afternoon and says He can't stand any more broken nights (not to mention broken teeth). He's not the only one.

Anyway, around ten o'clock She gave in. Managed to get a whole teaspoonful of sleeping draught down me. I can't have been concentrating.

# DAY 6

Woke up at half past three in the morning. Instantly started teething routine and continued throughout the day.

This time She only held out till nine o'clock in the evening. Two teaspoonfuls tonight.

Just before I drifted off to sleep, I heard the gratifying sounds of an argument from the bedroom. Couldn't hear the details, but I could hear Her say She was too tired.

The argument ended with the sound of Him stomping out and spending the night in the spare bedroom.

The power. I would have enjoyed it more if my gums weren't so sore.


# DAY 7

Woke three-thirty a.m., and started straight away.

She tottered into the nursery, looking more dead than alive, and gave me two more teaspoonfuls of the sleeping draught.

Back to sleep till six o'clock, then I started again.
Kept it up all day.

He came home from work absolutely exhausted, just managed to eat His supper and fell into bed at eight-thirty. In the spare room again.

At nine o'clock, She gave me three teaspoonfuls of the sleeping draught. I slept till a quarter to midnight, then the mayhem recommenced.

## DAY 8

Just after midnight, She gave me three more teaspoonfuls. I slept till three-thirty, when She gave me another three teaspoonfuls. I slept till six o'clock.

Rest of day spent as yesterday.

They're looking pretty flaked out now. Haven't heard any of this 'leading our own lives, in spite of the baby' rubbish from either of them for a while.

This evening I had six teaspoonfuls of the sleeping draught before midnight . . .

## DAY 9

. . . and six after midnight. Slept probably a total of three hours between the doses.

This evening She got all hysterical and started telling Him that it wasn't fair, at least He could get some sleep at the office, whereas She was going absolutely mad and not getting any. He was on the verge of making a jocular interpretation of the phrase 'not getting any', but, catching the look in Her eye, quickly thought better of it.

Instead, He got all solicitous and said that She should just go straight to bed and catch up on Her sleep, while He looked after me overnight.

Hm, I thought. If this is as successful as His other attempts at being a New Man . . .

He gave me ten teaspoonfuls of the sleeping draught before midnight . . .

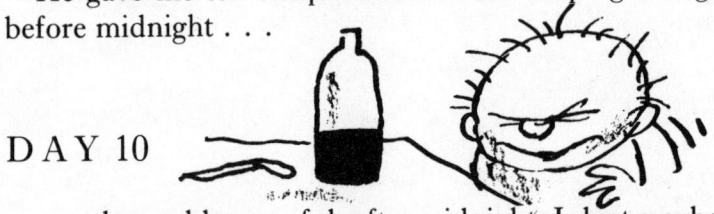

## DAY 10

. . . and ten tablespoonfuls after midnight. I slept maybe a couple of hours between these.

At four-thirty He got desperate and gave me a long sip from the whisky to which I had driven Him.

You know, I could get a taste for that stuff . . .

I slept till eleven o'clock in the morning, and woke up with my first hangover. This did not improve my behaviour during the day.

Still, to give Her Her due, She was very good. A full night's sleep had done wonders. Much less hysterical and really quite tolerant. She even said, after He had come home and eaten His supper and fallen into bed, that She'd just settle me and then 'join Him in a moment.'

I didn't have to be Sigmund Freud to read the subtext of that.

Of course I had to put a stop to it. Not difficult – I only had to delay Her in the nursery for ten minutes. By then He was comatose and He didn't emerge till morning.

She gave me the best part of a bottle of sleeping draught during the night . . .

## DAY 11

. . . but to little effect.

You see, since I've had that drop of whisky, the other stuff seems pretty tame.

Eventually, desperate to pacify me, She took me to bed with Her. This is something I have had in mind for nearly six months.

Trouble is, it was the spare-room bed. It's their bed that I really want to colonise. Give me time.

## DAY 12

Very nice waking up in Her arms. Must make it a habit.

He was not best pleased. He'd snuck into the spare room early in the morning and was pretty fazed to find me in there with Her.

He thought I was still asleep and snuggled up to Her, but that made Her very prudish. Apparently there's something in that book about it being a very bad idea for babies to see their parents doing certain things. Traumatic for their little psyches.

I'm not worried about my little psyche. But I am getting worried about His libido.

## DAY 13

Had my by-now-customary bottle of sleeping draught overnight, but still managed to be so inconsolable that She took me into the spare-room bed with Her. Very nice.

Also, in a nightdress my source of nourishment is just *so* accessible. Last night was spent in more or less continuous consumption. This is the life.


## DAY 14

Bottle of sleeping draught overnight, then an exciting new development – She took me into *their* bed!

He was asleep when She smuggled me in, but it didn't take me long to wake Him up.

Not very pleased to see me. After a bit of bad-tempered grunting and duvet-snatching, He retired defeated to the spare room.

My campaign is succeeding. After all, all I'm asking for is a little *Lebensraum*.


# DAY 16

A new variation on the sleeping arrangements. After my bottle of sleeping draught (which now has no more effect than a cup of water), She took me into their bed around four this morning.

He very quickly, without even token resistance, decamped to the spare room.

Then She, finding that I was twitching, grunting and spreading myself about too much, went through to join Him.

He predictably misinterpreted Her sudden appearance in His bed. There ensued a brief scuffle, at the end of which He stumped out of the spare room slamming the door, and made his way downstairs to the whisky bottle.

Glowing with the satisfaction of a job well done, I drifted off to sleep in my luxurious new territory.

The morning was quite funny. They both overslept. She, waking in the spare room, panicked that something might be wrong with me and rushed into their room to check I was OK.

Which of course I was. But I didn't let Her know that. Oh, no, I screamed and screamed until She fed me.

Then She suddenly realised She didn't know where He was. Carrying me (possetting merrily over Her shoulder), She started to search the house.

She finally came across Him crumpled up in my cot, and He took a lot of waking. Apparently, finding the whisky wasn't knocking Him out, around five-thirty He'd taken half a teaspoonful of my sleeping draught.

Twenty minutes it took Her to wake Him, and was He in a filthy temper? He left, late for work and breakfastless, skinning His shin against the gatepost on His way out, as we waved to Him from the window.

By the end of the day, the sleeping draught was still taking its toll. He'd kept walking into walls at the office. He fell asleep into His supper plate and She had to carry Him upstairs to bed.

So zonked out was He that He didn't even think about sex.

Oh, one interesting thing happened today. Mid-afternoon I suddenly noticed that the pain in my mouth had stopped, and that my lip kept catching on a funny little hard bit in my lower gums.

My first tooth was actually through!

This was brought forcibly to Her notice during my late-afternoon feed. Give Her Her due, She ignored the nip and expressed appropriate excitement.

'Ooh,' She burbled, 'oo's got a nice ickle tooth then? And now oo's going to sleep through the nights like a good ickle baby and not keep waking Mummy and Daddy up, isn't oo then?'

Sometimes she is just so naive.

# Seventh Month

## DAY 2

Now that I can more or less sit upright (when the mood takes me), She tends to feed me in the high chair in the kitchen. This has advantages and disadvantages. The disadvantage is that I get fewer opportunities for smearing food over Her clothes, engraining it into Her hair, etc., than I did when She used to feed me on Her lap.

On the other hand, the high chair has a nice little tray in front, perfect for rubbing food over with one's elbows, and a rail against which a spoon can be banged. Also, because of its height, it does offer an ideal throwing point for an upturned bowl of gunge.

Anyway, this evening, at the end of my teatime feed, I was about to do my customary posset (these days I just do it for form's sake – for a long time She's been too canny to get caught in the firing line) when I suddenly got caught by the most enormous and totally unexpected burp.

This had a rather dramatic effect. The contents of my 'posset' shot a good eighteen inches away from the high chair and landed with a satisfying 'splat' on the kitchen floor!

She reacted as She always does when I do something new, and scurried off to find the book.

Imagine Her delight, then, when she found a description in the index of something called 'projectile vomiting'. That's exactly what it was.

## DAY 3

Spent the day working out ways to perfect this great new trick.

This evening I managed to project the entire contents of my mouth *two feet* away from my high chair.

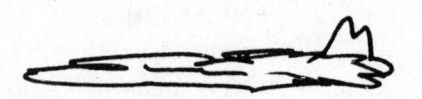

## DAY 4

At teatime, projectile vomit reached Her kitchen work surface for the first time – that has got to be a minimum of *two feet three inches* from the high chair – and got the cat straight between the eyes.

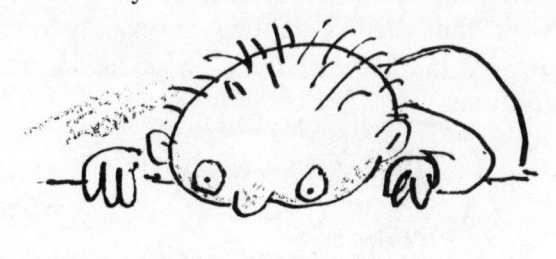

## DAY 5

Today, got as far as the cooker. *Two and a half feet* at least. Front of the cooker needed cleaning. Not bad.

## DAY 7

*Three foot* barrier breached! Yes, my personal best so far – actually got all the way to the kitchen door.

What made the record even better was the fact that He was walking through the door at the time. Had to change His jeans and trainers.

I wonder . . . what the chances are of projectile vomiting being admitted as an Olympic Sport by the time I'm old enough to compete?

If it is, the gold medal's in the bag.

# DAY 10

Today She took me to the swimming pool with a friend of Hers who also has a baby. They've been putting a lot of pressure on us recently to 'be friends', although it should be obvious that we can't stand each other.

For example, on the way to the pool when I was (reluctantly) sitting in my car seat and the friend sat cradling her baby in the back, I got all the 'Oh look, your baby's trying to reach out and touch my baby' (that bit was true) and 'Oo wants to give oo's friend a big kiss, doesn't oo?' (That bit wasn't true. All I wanted to do was knock oo's friend's block off.)

But they just couldn't understand this, and kept burbling on about what 'good friends' we'd be when we were older. Honestly, when I *do* come to have friends, why should I listen to my parents' advice about choosing them? Every other decision they've taken has been wrong. I mean, look at the name they chose for me . . .

I was given another example of Her lack of judgement even as I sat there. 'Have you thought about when you'll be going back to work?' Her friend asked.

And She had the nerve to reply, 'I'm hoping to get back part-time in a couple of months.'

Thanks for the warning, Mum. We'll see about that.

Swimming is actually quite fun. Good opportunities for flicking water in Her face. Of course I can actually float, but every time She risked letting go of me, I sank to the bottom like a stone. It was worth doing just for the expression on Her face as She dragged me back to the surface.

# DAY 13

As a result of my swimming expedition, I now have a streaming cold. Something very satisfying about trailing a long tendril of snot everywhere I go. Also enjoy grinding it into Her shoulder, the carpet, the furniture, the wall-paper, etc.

I was given my first book today. Hadn't got any words in it, just the alphabet with brightly coloured pictures.

'There, oo's got a uvvy big book then?' She cooed. (I do wish She'd stop asking these rhetorical questions. It's perfectly obvious to the meanest intellect oo's got a uvvy big book if you ask the question of the person oo – I mean *who* you've just given it to.)

'Is oo going to read oo's uvvy big book then?' She went on, and left me alone with it.

I didn't read the book. You can't read pictures, can you?

But I did rip the cover off, tear out four pages and chew three others. I ate A for apple, B for ball . . . they tasted just like those jars of soggy cardboard I keep being given.

## DAY 16

Yet another innovation in my life. A friend of Hers who's had lots of babies has passed on a playpen. I can't say I like the look of it.

It's pretty ancient: a horrible great wooden thing with bars from which all the paint has been sucked off – by previous inmates, I imagine.

So far She's only shown it to me. 'Oo's got a uvvy new playpen then? Doesn't oo love oo's uvvy ickle playpen then?'

As with every new thing in my life, I greeted it with such vociferous screams that She didn't even dare put me down inside it.

But I know Her – She'll keep on trying.

## DAY 17

Sure enough, She put me in the playpen this morning.

I screamed, trying to tell Her that I was too young to be seeing the world through bars, but as usual She misunderstood the point I was trying to make.

'Yes, it must be frustrating for oo, mustn't it then?' She

said. 'Oo'll like oo's playpen better when oo can move around in it, won't oo then?'

Fat chance.

One wall of the playpen has a kind of mini-abacus of coloured plastic beads set into it. As She was lifting me out, I stretched out a hand to these and She encouraged me to play with them. 'Does oo want to play with oo's uvvy ickle rattly beads then?'

No, I didn't want to play with them. I just wanted to see how secure they were, and was pleased to find they felt very loose in their mounting. So did the supporting bars on either side.

I'll bear this in mind in case a breakout from the playpen ever becomes necessary.

# DAY 18

The playpen has been stowed away in the cupboard under the stairs, but I am not fooled by this. I know they will bring it back again some time, and when they do, I'll be ready for it!

# DAY 21

I have developed a new trick – supporting myself on both knees and only one hand. My parents are more impressed by this breakthrough than I am. It must be of some use, but I haven't yet worked out what.

# DAY 22

Got it! I can now keep myself steady while grabbing things I couldn't reach before. Brilliant!

Left alone in the kitchen after breakfast, I managed to open the saucepan cupboard with my free hand and pull all the saucepans out on to the floor. Sadly nothing actually broken, but none the less a very satisfying noise.

She was divided between admiration at my prowess and annoyance at the mess I had made.

# DAY 23

Another triumph for my one-hand trick.

Left alone in the sitting room after my rest, I managed to pull all the ornaments off the bottom shelves. Not everything broke, but still a very creditable first attempt.

> SCORE: 3 china figurines
> 2 souvenir jugs bought on their honeymoon in Majorca
> 1 engraved wineglass given to Her on Her twenty-first

(Unfortunately discovered that the china figurines were wedding presents from His godfather that they'd never liked and were glad to see the back of. Better luck next time.)

This time She was rather less divided between admiration at my prowess and annoyance at the mess I had made.

## DAY 24

Still refining my one-handed trick.

Left alone in my parents' bedroom while She answered the telephone, I managed to open Her wardrobe door and pull down loads of Her clothes. A good few ripped.

> SCORE: (TORN) 3 dresses, 2 skirts, 1 silk jacket
> (SLOBBERED OVER) 2 dresses, 1 suit, 1 pair of leggings, 2 pairs of jeans

She showed no admiration at my prowess, but a good deal of tearful annoyance at the mess I had made.

## DAY 25

Another one-handed triumph.

Left alone in His study, I managed to pull all the books out of the bottom two shelves of the bookcase in which He keeps His modern First Editions (a collection inherited from His grandfather).

Discovered that, just like my big picture book, grown-up books have easily detachable covers and pages that tear.

SCORE: 2 James Bonds
1 Graham Greene
1 Kingsley Amis

He had *no* problem deciding between admiration at my prowess and annoyance at the mess I had made.


# DAY 27

He really has got a one-track mind. This evening He was trying again. From my cot I could hear mumbles and a rustling of fabric in the bedroom.

'Hm, they still look pretty good,' He was murmuring.

For a moment I wondered what He was on about, but Her next words narrowed down the options.

'They should settle down when I stop breastfeeding.'

Then I heard Him say, 'When *are* you going to stop breastfeeding? The solids seem to be going down very well, if the evidence over the furniture and wallpaper is anything to go by.'

'Well,' She replied judiciously, 'I plan to start weaning next month . . .'

Oh, does She? We'll see about that.

' . . . I mean, it'll be gradual. May take a couple of months to get baby off the breast completely . . .'

Don't you believe it. Couple of *years* will be nearer the mark.

I allowed them another minute then let out the first Oh-my-God-it-might-be-meningitis bellow.

# *Eighth Month*

## DAY 1

Got another new trick. I've been able to pick objects up between thumb and forefinger for a few weeks, but now I'm managing to exert a bit of pressure. In fact, I can make my fingers act just like a little vice.

At first they were very impressed. 'Oh, look how tightly oo's holding that then! Isn't óo a clever ickle baby then?' (How I'm ever going to learn to talk properly when all I hear is that kind of gibberish, God knows.)

They were less impressed when they realised that, once having grasped an object in my vice-like fingers, there was no way I was going to let it go.

The new trick really comes into its own at mealtimes. If I get a fruit or vegetable in my hand, it's only a matter of moments before I've squidged it into a pulpy mess ideal for smearing on walls, furniture, visitors, the cat, etc.

Terrific in the supermarket, too. From my throne at the end of the trolley, I can easily reach down to all the stuff she's buying, grab hold and squeeze. Things like yoghurt and cheesepots are the best. The containers give token resistance for a while, but eventually burst open in a most satisfying way. I managed to get Apricot and Redcurrant Dessert over everything this morning.

The vice-like grip is also great on hair. He hasn't really got enough for me to get a good purchase, but Hers is ideal. I try to grab a handful every time She picks me up. Once I've got a good tight hold, there's no way I can let go.

Today I pulled out four decent-sized hanks.

Result is She's more paranoid than ever about Her appearance. Wide hips, stretch marks, increasingly floppy breasts . . . and now patchy hair. Notice I'm hearing less these days about not allowing having had a baby to change Her life.

## DAY 2

Got the cat's tail in my vice-like grip this morning. It was not happy.

However, what She'd said about all the ghastly things that'd happen if it ever scratched me again have obviously sunk in and it offered no resistance, just yowled pitifully.

After about twenty minutes, She became aware of the noise and came in to see what was going on. I ungripped my fingers just in time (haven't managed to do that before) and started screaming. The cat didn't even wait to be blamed but shot straight out through the cat-flap and hasn't reappeared. That was close.

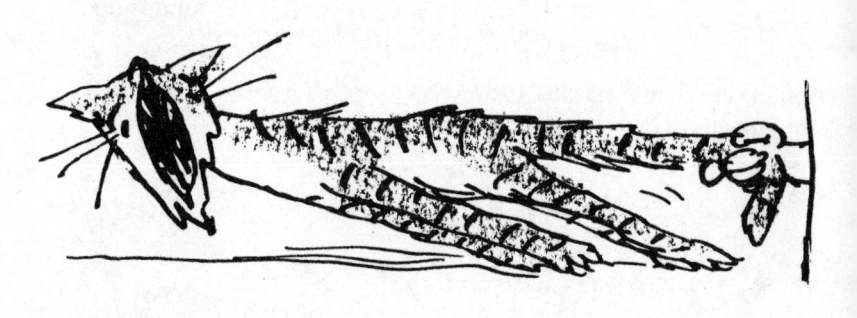

# DAY 4

Woke up early this morning and was just about to let out my customary summoning bellow when I heard my parents talking. And for a change it wasn't anything to do with sex.

It was about me, of course.

'I'm going to start today,' She announced.

'Start what?' He asked blearily.

'Weaning.' I was instantly alert. 'I'm going to cut out the midday feeds. Just breast in the morning and last thing at night, and then a bottle with the other meals.'

We'll see about that.

My objection to being weaned is not that I don't like the bottle. I've had it on and off since my first month, and actually quite enjoy the taste of the stuff.

No, what I object to is the challenge weaning represents to my power-base. The concept of a free-ranging mother – even, Heaven forbid, a working mother – who can leave me alone for long periods is very different from the current situation of a woman virtually chained to me by having to breastfeed at every meal.

So, I'm afraid this weaning idea is doomed to failure until – probably in two or three years' time – I find that the constant feeding interferes with *my* social life and *I* make the decision to put a stop to it.

However, I didn't let on that I knew what was happening – rather the reverse; after only a few seconds at the breast, I appeared to lose interest and at breakfast wolfed down several dishes of soggy cardboard cereal.

It was at lunchtime that She got Her come-uppance. When I was offered a bottle rather than a breast after my jar of Lamb and Spinach (I think – it's hard to tell), I raised the roof.

And I managed, through my tears, to contrive an expression of bewildered reproach. As ever, emotional blackmail paid off and I was on the breast within five minutes.

She made another feeble attempt at teatime, but caved in even quicker.

That night, from my cot I heard with satisfaction as She

said to Him, 'No, I'm afraid it's too soon for weaning just yet. I think we'll have to give it another couple of months.'

Game to me, I think.

| Me | 36 |
|-----|----|
| Her | 2 |

# DAY 6

One thing that's touching about them is the way they imagine they understand what I'm thinking, even though they're nearly always one hundred per cent wrong.

For instance, this evening the two of them arrived for a goodnight coo over my cot. It was still light, and they could see my eyes fixed on that hideous mobile of fluffy crocodiles that's been the bane of my life for the last seven months.

She murmured winsomely, 'Doesn't oo love oo's uvvy ickle crocodiles then?'

I don't know. I can see why there's a long tradition of conflict and misunderstanding between the generations. Parents are just so BLOODY STUPID.

## DAY 8

Major visit to the clinic today for my Eight Month Assessment Test.

This morning at breakfast I was sitting on the floor by the kitchen table when I heard Her talking to Him about it. 'Don't think we'll have any problems,' She said airily. 'Baby's development is exactly as it should be, according to my childcare book.'

'Good,' He said absently from behind His paper.

'And I'm not going to be put off by what happened last time. I'm definitely going to have another go at weaning soon.'

'Good,' He said.

'So I should be able to go back to work part-time – just as we planned.'

I don't know. When will they realise that these days I'm the one who does the planning round here?

I had to think fast and came up with a plan which I put into action immediately, by falling heavily against the kitchen table leg. This produced exactly what I had intended – a bleeding lip and a bruise the size of a golf ball on my temple. Clever stuff.

Had to wait quite a while in the waiting room when we got to the clinic. I passed the time by sitting up straight, waving my hands around, picking up objects from the floor in my vice-like grip, banging on things and making little gurgly noises that sounded almost like speech.

Then we got inside and saw the doctor. I went totally silent and listless, while She propped me up on the table.

The doctor took one look at me and reacted exactly as I'd hoped. 'How did the baby get that bruise on its forehead and the split lip?'

'Fell against the kitchen table,' She replied, sounding very guilty.

'I *see*,' said the doctor, mentally marking his card. 'Well, how about basic developmental skills? Can the baby sit up unaided?'

'Yes, of course,' She replied, removing the support of Her hands.

I keeled slowly over on to my side.

'I *see*,' said the doctor once again. 'Well, we'd better test the hearing.'

I must admit it wasn't easy keeping a straight face. There's something deeply silly about a grown man moving round the room whispering at you from lots of different positions. And it's hard not to react when he's reduced to putting his lips right up against your ear and bellowing.

But I didn't crack. Not the tiniest flinch. I just lay there silent and listless until he let out another 'I *see*' and wrote something down on his clipboard.

And what the doctor thought he was doing waving silly coloured objects at me and constantly popping his head round the corner of things, I just don't know. But again I was perfect – just lay there, gazing listlessly ahead.

'I *see*.' More notes were confided to the clipboard.

It was the same when he tried to get me to pick things up. I resisted the temptation to seize all the little objects that were pushed towards me, and continued staring apathetically.

'Normally very good at this,' She said nervously. 'Picks up everything. It's this month's new trick.'

The doctor gave Her a long slow look. Though I say it myself, the bruise and the split lip had really been a brainwave. No chance he was going to believe anything She said after he'd seen those.

He finally abandoned trying to get a response out of me, and concentrated on Her. I'm sorry to say She left the clinic in tears.

Cruel, you may say, but I had to put a stop to all this talk of Her returning to work part-time. And I think I've managed that.

To cheer Her up in the car on the way home, I sat up straight, waved my hands around, picked up everything within reach in my vice-like grip, banged on things and made little gurgling noises that sounded almost like speech.

# DAY 14

I've been experimenting with this moving about lark, and have to report some good news and some bad news.

The good news is that I have achieved movement – i.e., after considerable effort, I have managed to end up in a position different from the one in which I started.

The bad news, however, is that I don't seem to have any control over the direction in which I go.

I must continue to work on this. I've got to the stage now where I've destroyed everything I can actually reach, and my parents are getting cannier about leaving me in the middle of rooms rather than on the outskirts, near shelves, cupboards, etc.

So, if I'm going to continue the swathe of domestic destruction I have in mind, learning to move's a top priority.

# DAY 15

I do hate people watching me while I'm trying something new.

It happened this afternoon. I was on the sitting-room floor having another go at moving about. I had tried raising myself on my hands and knees, but it's actually a lot harder than it sounds.

Then I just lifted my upper body on my hands, and tried rocking the rest of me into motion. This did result in a bit of geographical relocation, but again the direction in which I moved was totally random.

In fact, worse than random, it was exactly the opposite direction to the one I wanted. I'd got my eye on a tray of glasses She'd left on the floor. She'd been about to put them away when the phone rang and I was itching to go across and smash them up.

Imagine my fury when I found all my efforts were getting me further away from the glasses rather than nearer. I was actually going backwards!

The sound of a little giggle from the doorway did not help matters. Craning my head round, I saw Her peering through the crack of the door and actually laughing at me.

How could She?!

## DAY 16

Lay in my cot this morning wondering whether I was right to expend so much energy on trying to move about. Perhaps I should concentrate on another developmental achievement – talking, for instance.

Talking is clearly going to be very handy. Quite like the idea of being able to *tell* them what I think of their behaviour rather than just expressing my disagreement by screams and bowel movements.

But a few minutes' thought decided me against it. If I did suddenly start talking, they'd make SUCH A FUSS.

Already She monitors my every tiny advance by comparing me with the all-purpose standard baby in that book. If I did something really out of sequence like talking at eight months, I'd never hear the end of it.

She'd be convinced they'd spawned a genius; there'd be consultations with child psychologists and educationalists and associations for parents of gifted children . . . and, quite honestly, I don't think I could cope with the hassle.

No. I'll stick to being ordinary – just do what sensible babies have done for generations, and develop at the pace parents generally expect. Anything for a quiet life.


## DAY 27

Control over movement improving. I can now, using both my hands and sort of pivoting on my bottom, move more or less in the direction that I want to. It's not easy, it's certainly not elegant, but I'll stick at it. Opportunities for mischief are going to be very limited until I can get about properly.


## DAY 28

Actually managed to move myself far enough across the room to pull the wire of a table lamp and bring it crashing down to the floor. Unfortunately the stand didn't break, but I comforted myself with the thought that the bulb was probably done for.

Stupidly, I stayed where I was, on the floor beside the lamp, so that when She came into the sitting room She could see exactly what had happened. She told me I was a naughty baby, then replaced the lamp on its table and tested the switch. To my annoyance, the light came on.

## DAY 29

A much more successful exercise in destruction this morning. The cat was lying on the sitting-room sofa as I wormed my way towards the table on which a glass vase of flowers stood.

Once beside the table, I grabbed one of the legs and started to shake it fiercely. The operation took a while, but the vase edged inch by inch along the table-top until eventually it toppled off. There was a satisfying sound of breaking glass, as flowers and water spread all over the carpet.

I then managed to get to the other side of the room in my fastest time yet, where I picked up a rattle in the shape of a lollipop; She's been trying to get me interested in it for at least five months so I felt now was a good time to try it. I put it in my mouth and started to chew.

The timing was tight. I'd only just got into position when She came in. The sight of the broken vase really got Her livid, and She looked indecisively between me and the cat.

I'm delighted to say She reached the right conclusion.

The cat was fiercely smacked until it broke free and hurtled out of the cat-flap for yet another supperless night of feeling misunderstood.

Tee-hee.

# Ninth Month

## DAY 5

I decided this morning that I haven't been making nearly enough fuss about getting dressed.

I can't believe it's taken me so long to realise this. After all, I've made a fuss about getting into the car seat ever since it was introduced into my life – in fact for that I've perfected what I call the 'Starfish Position'.

The Starfish Position, if you will forgive me going off at a slight tangent, is very simple – just a matter of straightening the spine as rigidly as possible and extending both arms and legs outwards to form a Maltese cross shape, which is almost impossible to fit into the straps.

Anyway, from now on I am going to develop a similar technique to resist getting dressed. It's just a matter of ensuring that no limb goes straight into the garment's hole towards which the parent is trying to guide it, and that any limb which does inadvertently end up down a sleeve or trouser-leg is removed as quickly as possible (ideally with enough twisting and turning to get the garment into a hopeless tangle).

This process should be accompanied by as much screaming, dribbling, possetting and scratching as possible.

I must say, it worked a treat this morning. Dressing me, which till now She's always done inside five minutes, took twenty.

And I think, if I really work on my technique, I could soon get it up to the full half-hour. Maybe even longer.

But you've always got to be one step ahead: carry on with this infuriating behaviour for too long and you'll find your parents will start to use increasing force in their efforts to get you into your clothes.

And, when it comes to a contest of pure strength, they are going to win. They're bigger than you, they're stronger than you, and there's not much you can do about it.

One thing you can do, though, is to ensure that you make them think they've REALLY HURT YOU. Redouble your screams as the final limb is thrust into its destination, and simultaneously make it go limp. If they try to get movement from it, keep it limp, but make sure you scream in agony every time it's touched.

Parents have very little basic confidence. They're easily rattled, and their minds will quickly fill with visions of having to take you to hospital, of the disbelieving looks on the faces of the doctors, and of the hordes of suspicious social workers who will descend on their house in order to put you on the 'at risk' register. (Remember how successful my behaviour at the Eight Month Test was.)

Yes, you can really scare the pants off your parents – no problem.

## DAY 10

Her friend and baby – you know, the two I went swimming with – turned up again today. The two mothers are still pathetically keen that we should be 'friends'.

Things have improved since our last encounter, though. My new mobility enables me to get close enough to have a good go at knocking the little beast's block off. They didn't stay long.

Apparently, according to Her, who likes putting names to things, and likes it even better when those names correspond to entries in the famous index of that book, my current mode of movement is known as 'bottom-shuffling'.

Funny, I'd always thought that was a way of cheating at cards.

## DAY 11

Today something I've been dreading for quite some time happened, which resulted in the loss of my hard-fought liberty. She got the playpen out from the cupboard under the stairs, and put me in it.

I screamed my head off, but to no avail.

## DAY 12

Incarcerated in the playpen again this morning.

It is inhuman to detain anyone without trial in a space only four foot by four foot.

I wonder how you get in touch with Amnesty International.

## DAY 14

Ignored the plastic toys, rattles and general rubbish my captor threw into my cell for me to play with, and concentrated instead on the abacus of beads attached to the playpen wall. Pulled and rattled at them all morning.

They're getting looser. It's going to be a long job, but I will persevere.

Would form an escape committee, but it seems a bit daft since I'd be the only member. Perhaps I should invite the cat to join.

## DAY 16

Thoughts of escape from the playpen have been diverted by the development of a new skill.

I've suddenly found I can poke my fingers into things. Or, to be more accurate, I can poke *a* finger into things.

It came to me in a flash. When She picked me out of my cot this morning, I poked my finger in Her eye.

She took a dim view of this, so I poked my finger in Her other eye, which made Her view even dimmer.

## DAY 17

Poked finger in His eye.

## DAY 18

Poked finger in cat's eye. Ruined my chances of getting it to join the escape committee.

## DAY 19

Poked finger in Her mother's eye.

Effect greatly enhanced by the fact that He laughed when I did it. Atmosphere between Her mother and Him even frostier than usual.

## DAY 20

Tried to poke finger in electrical socket, but was dragged away by Her, screaming all kinds of dreadful things.

I will try again next time Her back is turned.

95

# DAY 22

Took my lately acquired skill of picking up tiny objects to new heights today. This afternoon I was in Her bedroom, while She was changing Her clothes after a particularly messy lunchtime, when there was a ring at the front door.

She shot off downstairs, because the washing machine's broken and She thought it might be the repairman.

(Since my arrival, the washing machine breaking down has taken on the aspect of a national disaster. The speed with which I soil my clothes and those of anyone within reach – particularly because I'm still a virtuoso projectile vomiter – ensures that She does about four loads a day. When the machine's not working, it only takes a few hours for Her to be up to here in filthy washing.)

Anyway, it *was* the repairman, so She ushered him into the kitchen to assess the damage, leaving me to my own devices. My devices in this particular instance involved bottom-shuffling towards the dressing-table, on which her jewellery box lay open.

I pulled myself up against the stool on which She sits to do Her makeup (on the rare occasions that I leave Her time to put on any makeup). I was too far away to reach the box itself, but I did manage to grab at a string of little round glass beads.

My hand closed and I got a firm grip, but something seemed to be anchoring them to the dressing-table. I tugged, but to no avail.

It was at this moment I lost my balance. Though I'm getting better at this standing-up business, I'm still pretty unstable, particularly when supporting myself on only one hand. So I sort of swivelled round on the hand that clasped the dressing-table and subsided gracefully, landing on my bottom.

The bonus was that my other hand was still clutching the beads. Unequal to the weight of my body, the string snapped and the tiny glass balls pattered down on to the carpet.

I scrabbled around on the floor, picking them up between my thumb and forefinger and wondered what to do with them. Tried throwing a bead against the wall. It hit it with a satisfying ping. Good game.

I had probably been playing it for five minutes when She came in. I looked up at Her winsomely, my right hand firmly placed in my mouth.

She shrieked. 'Oh no! You haven't! You haven't put any in your mouth, have you?'

I continued to look winsome. She snatched my hand from my mouth and found it was empty. I screamed, partly because I didn't like having my hand snatched away, and partly to add to the dramatic atmosphere. I've always had a strong sense of theatre.

'Oh, my God!' She went on, dropping to Her knees to pick up the beads. 'Have you put any of them in your mouth?'

I screamed louder, to match Her level of panic.

She continued Her frantic picking up of the beads. 'How many were there? How many were there?' She kept moaning.

She checked the beads against the length of string, and came to a conclusion which seemed to upset Her even more.

She picked me up and started banging my back. I redoubled the volume of my screams, in that special way which makes me go purple in the face.

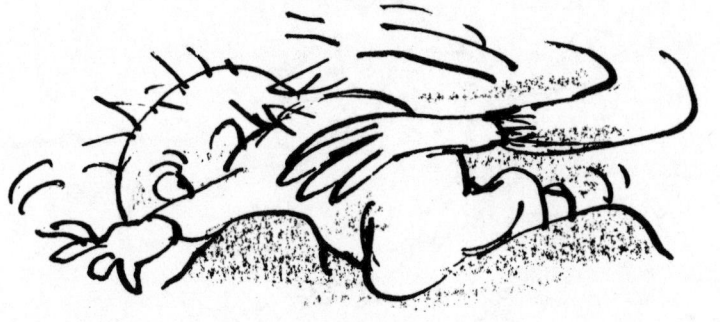

Clutching me to Her, She rushed downstairs to ring the doctor and, within minutes it seemed, an ambulance had arrived at the house.

Inside the ambulance, I suddenly stopped screaming and went quiet; all the excitement had made me feel quite sleepy. This seemed to worry them even more.

Well, you know what hospitals are like. There was a lot of waiting and a lot of rushing about before I finally got to be X-rayed. I passed the time by alternately screaming

myself purple and going quiet. This seemed to keep the surrounding anxiety level satisfyingly high.

The X-rays revealed nothing, but it was decided I should be kept in overnight for observation.

# DAY 23

I wasn't aware of any hospital staff around observing me. The people who did all the observation seemed to be Him and Her.

If I'd ever had any doubts about the extent of my power over them (which of course I never had), the expressions on their faces that night would have dispelled them.

In the morning I was given a desultory examination by a doctor (who seemed totally uninterested), and discharged. But all day at home She kept looking at me, as if She was afraid I might suddenly vanish in a puff of smoke.

I suppose one day She'll find the glass beads I pushed under the edge of the carpet.

## Tenth Month

### DAY 1

It suddenly struck me this morning that today is a great watershed in my life. It's over nine months since I was born. In other words, I've been longer out than in.

Upturned a plate of Beef and Vegetable dinner over the cat, so that the day didn't pass completely uncelebrated.

### DAY 3

Confined to playpen for an inhuman length of time again today. Continued working away at abacus bit and adjacent bars.

It won't be long now. But I mustn't even think about it. After a lengthy period of imprisonment, it's all too easy to get 'stir crazy'.

### DAY 5

One thing my parents have been talking about on and off over the last nine months is holidays.

Apparently these used to be the high spots of their childless years. It seems they were always buzzing off somewhere hot, like Greece or Spain, to spend a fortnight lying in the sun, swimming and drinking, interrupting this pattern only for frequent returns to their villa for long siestas (or, at least, that's what they called them).

It sounds like a pretty decadent way of life, and certainly not one they'll be able to pick up again now I'm around.

To give them their due, they seem to have accepted that; She more readily than He. 'It's really not going to be much fun going abroad until the baby's older,' She's been saying. 'In a few years we can start having foreign holidays again.'

He always follows this remark with a gloomy 'If we can afford it.'

He is coming to realise that my arrival has not only brought a little sunshine into His life, it has also brought a considerable increase in expenditure.

Actually, so far as expense is concerned, I've hardly started. I have chosen not to talk yet, and I watch very little television. Just let them wait till I can articulate my demands for all the expensive things I see advertised on the box.

And just let them wait till I start school and the 'All the other kids have got them – why can't I have one?' routine.

But to return to the subject of holidays . . . As I say, they've come to terms, more or less grudgingly, with the idea that they can't go abroad this year, but they are still thinking of 'taking some time off in this country'.

'After all,' I overheard Her saying this evening, 'we've had a tiring year. We could really both do with a rest.'

I can guarantee that, whatever they do get, it won't be a rest.

# DAY 7

They've progressed a bit on the holiday front. He's booked some leave for the week after next, and She got some brochures at the travel agent for holidays in Britain.

They spent a dispiriting evening going through them. Almost every kind of break He fancied (mostly ones that involved hang gliding, rock climbing, parachuting . . . ) had to be ruled out because the places didn't take children.

The ones She fancied (those with a really elaborate cuisine – she's a bit of a frustrated gastronome on the quiet) had to be ruled out for the same reason.

At the end of the evening, they looked at each other in abject misery.

If nothing else had done it, that moment brought home to them the full depressing truth of how much my arrival has changed their lives.

# DAY 8

A major breakthrough. After some weeks of bottom-shuffling round my playpen, I decided to experiment with a different form of locomotion.

I started from a flat-on-the-tummy position, then raised my head and torso with the support of my arms. Next I tried lifting my stomach from the floor by moving my knees.

The first few attempts were not very efficient. In fact, they were rather painful because I kept dive-bombing forward on to my nose.

But I kept trying and eventually was rewarded by a degree of success. Probably moved forward a few inches. Left it at that for today, though. Don't want to run before I can walk – or do I mean walk before I can crawl . . . ?

## DAY 9

Went on practising my new movement technique. In secret. I stopped every time I heard Her coming into the room. Don't want Her to be aware of the stage management this time. Just want to present Her with the finished product.

## DAY 10

Stupid. I let Her creep up on me this morning.

She was very chuffed by what she saw. 'Oh, is oo crawling then?' She warbled. 'Is oo a clever big crawling baby then?'

I played up to Her uncomplicated delight. What else could I do?

She instantly rang Her mother to share the glad tidings. Their conversation started on a mellow note, but then soured. It seems Her mother's response to the news was something along the lines of: 'Oh well, now that baby's doing that, the next thing you'll be concentrating on will be toilet training, won't it?'

From Her reaction, I gather that toilet training is another point of dissension between the generations. Great, I can use that.

She didn't ring Him up with the news. Decided to surprise Him when He came home from the office.

He came back in a filthy temper. He's having to work extra-hard to get everything tied up before our impending holiday.

Perhaps for that reason, He seemed pretty underwhelmed with my latest achievement.

'Guess what, darling?' She enthused as He came through the front door. 'The baby's crawling!!!'

'Oh,' said He sourly. 'What with?'

## DAY 13

I was a bit careless today. Preoccupied with other thoughts – like my plans for the Great Playpen Escape and the potential for chaos and mayhem offered by our forthcoming holiday – I let Her slip something past me.

I wasn't concentrating after lunch, or again after tea, and it was only when I heard Her making an announcement to Him after I'd been put to bed that I realised what I'd done wrong.

'Baby took a bottle instead of the breast twice today,' She said proudly. 'After lunch and after tea. I knew it was just a matter of waiting. So, as of today, we can officially say that we've started weaning!'

I must immediately initiate a rearguard action to recover the ground I have lost.

## DAY 14

She is getting more cunning. Frustrated my immediate response to the weaning offensive by going out for most of the day and leaving me – as well as all the hardware of bottlefeeding – with Her mother. So I had little alternative after lunch and supper but to wrap my lips around the alien teat.

And then, to make things worse, at bedtime when I was really gasping for a good slurp, Her breasts hardly produced anything.

'Sorry,' She announced smugly. 'You see, now you're being grown-up and getting weaned, the supply's drying up.'

There's something dodgy going on. Bet She snuck into the bathroom just before my feed and expressed most of the contents of Her breasts down the plug-hole.

I don't like having my authority challenged in this way.

## DAY 15

She is proving very stubborn. Offered me the bottle after both meals again today and, in spite of some real Oscar-winning howls of distress, resolutely refused to unbutton for me.

It makes it even more galling to know that, without the stimulus of regular sucking, Her milk supply is diminishing all the time.

I must find a way round this problem.

## DAY 17

This evening He came home from work even more harrassed than usual. It was His last day before our long-awaited holiday. He'd been frantically busy, and all He wanted to do was to dive into a large whisky.

But She said no, they should pack the car first. It would only take a minute, then He could have a nice relaxed drink.

With bad grace, He said all right. His grace did not improve one bit when He saw the mass of gear piled up in the spare room.

'Bloody hell!' he said. 'We're going on a week's holiday, not opening a branch of Mothercare!'

She then took Him through the stuff, item by item, and explained exactly why every last bit was needed. It was all for me, of course.

First, there was practically every garment I possess. 'Babies do get through an incredible number of clothes, and hotel laundries can be very expensive.'

Then there were enough boxes of disposable nappies to build a small town. 'We don't know how near the hotel is to the shops – it'd be dreadful to run out.'

There was another small townsworth of boxes of nappy liners, baby wipes and tissues.

There was enough cotton wool to be mistaken in the

dark for a flock of sheep.

There was a small trunk of medicines for the treatment of acne, allergic rhinitis, alopecia areata, angio-neurotic oedema, athlete's foot, bites, blackheads, blocked tear-duct, boils, bronchitis, bruises, burns, chickenpox, chilblains, cholera, colds, cold sores, conjunctivitis, constipation, convulsions, coughs, croup, cradle cap, cuts, dandruff, dermatitis, diarrhoea, ear-ache, eczema, folliculitis, grazes, groin rash, heat rash, heatstroke, herpes, hookworm, hives, impetigo, influenza, jaundice, laryngitis, malaria, measles, mercury poisoning, mumps, nappy rash, nettle rash, obstruction of the bowel, pigeon toes, pink eye, prickly heat, psittacosis, ringworm, scabies, scurvy, septic spots, shingles, sinusitis, smallpox, sore throat, stings, strabismus, streptococcus, styes, tapeworm, threadworm, thrush, tonsillitis, urticaria, verruca, warts, whooping cough and yellow fever.

There was also a carrycot plus wheels, a baby buggy, a playpen and a collapsible cot.

'Oh dear,' said He, his voice heavy with sarcasm. 'Why don't we take the kitchen sink while we're at it?'

'Thank goodness you reminded me!' said She, as ever impervious to irony. 'I forgot the baby bath!'

They finally got the car packed at half past one.

There wasn't room in it for any of *their* stuff.

# DAYS 18–24

Our week's holiday was an unparallelled disaster.

At least from their point of view. I quite enjoyed it.

I mean it's fun seeing how long you have to scream in an unfamiliar hotel room before people start knocking on the walls. Or how many things you have to knock over in a restaurant before you're asked to leave.

My parents got no peace, no sleep and certainly no time together both alone *and* awake.

Also it rained more or less continuously.

One new experience. During a brief break between downpours, I was taken on to the beach.

Since it was a bleak, windswept beach, I didn't care for it much. The only interesting fact I found out about beaches was that wet sand looks exactly like all the beige soggy confections I get at mealtimes.

So I ate a lot of sand. Didn't taste that different either.

I also used my new skill of crawling, while their backs were turned, to reach bits of seaweed, shreds of polythene bags and dog turds, which I wouldn't have been able to reach if we'd gone on holiday a month earlier.

So I ate a lot of those, too.

One positive achievement did come out of the week, however. She had to spend so much time calming me at the breast that Her milk supply is once again copious and abundant.

No more talk of weaning, or returning to work part-time, I'm glad to say.

# Eleventh Month

## DAY 7

Why are they both so inconsistent? First they encourage me to do things, and then suddenly they stop.

For example, ever since my first efforts in crawling, they've encouraged me to continue with it and seem pleased with my progress. But then, every time I go into the hall and start making for the stairs, they grab hold and stop me.

This is very short-sighted. They seem terribly keen for me to be good at everything in later life, but they should realise you don't produce Renaissance Men and Women by stopping them going upstairs!

## DAY 11

All that head-banging against the side of my playpen finally paid off today.

I'd been noticing for some weeks that the little abacus bit had been getting looser and looser.

Today I decided to put it to the test in that unguarded time while She hangs out the washing. (This usually takes ages as I'm still giving her at least three machine loads a day.)

After twenty minutes of sustained head-butting against the weakened side of the playpen, I tried taking hold of two of the bead-bearing wires and sitting down suddenly with all my weight.

I couldn't have asked for a better result. The wires sprang from their sockets and the beads scattered everywhere, mostly inside the playpen.

Flushed with success, I immediately pulled myself up and did the same thing to the remaining wire. Same result.

I reached out towards the two uprights that had had the beads between them. They too were gratifyingly loose. I was about to try my full weight against one of them, when caution prevailed.

Instead, I gathered up the scattered beads and hid them wherever possible. A few fitted neatly into my plastic toys, some I shoved under the rug, and others I managed to hurl across the room under the sofa.

I had barely hidden the last bead, and was about to have another go at the uprights, when She returned from the garden.

Immediately She noticed the gap where beads and wires had been, and went straight into panic mode, terrified once again that I'd swallowed them.

This was not what I'd intended, but it did have the advantage of distracting Her attention from the weakened state of the playpen wall.

It had the disadvantage, however, of pushing Her into the major hysteria She had manifested over Her glass beads a couple of months back.

I tried to point out the toys, the rug, the sofa, so that She could find the missing asphyxiators, but it was no good.

She insisted on going through the full hospital routine again (see NINTH MONTH – DAYS 22–23).

Which was really frustrating because it delayed the Great Playpen Escape.

# DAY 12

Didn't get back home from hospital till lunchtime.

And even then didn't get a chance to pursue escape plans. She was so worried after the bead panic that She insisted on carrying me round with Her all afternoon 'to see that I was all right'.

# DAY 13

She once again spent the entire day looking soulfully at me as if I was about to stage the Death of Little Nell and She was lucky still to have me. I suppose such attention is flattering, but I wish She'd just put me in the playpen and let me get on with my escape!

# DAY 17

Thank goodness, today I was once again incarcerated in my prison and was able to put my long-nursed plan into action.

Yes, today was the day of the Great Playpen Escape.

Whole thing went a dream. Absolutely tickety-boo, wilko, Roger-and-out.

Started at ten-hundred hours when guard out on hanging-up-washing fatigue. Approached suspect section of playpen wall, took firm grasp of upright in both hands, leant back with full weight, subsided to sitting position.

No good. Undeterred, tried again. This time, slight shift and creak from wood.

Third time – perfect. Part splintered off horizontal bar at top, vertical bar came free, fell back into playpen. Still attached at bottom, but few moments wrestling pulled it free.

Tried aperture, but still too narrow to admit plump baby in disposable nappy and tracksuit.

Turned attention to second upright. More rigid than first, but gave at sixth attempt. Also worked free from bottom horizontal.

Tried aperture. Tight, but managed to wriggle free.

Liberty! Tasted pretty good, I can tell you!

Moment of indecision about what to do now I was out,

but there could really only be one objective. Crawled across sitting-room floor and into hall. Made for stairs.

Never done stairs before, but didn't let that slow me down. Don't know what you can do till you try. Put hands on second step, eased knees up on to first. Moved hands up to third step, knees up to second, and so on.

Piece of cake. Don't know what all the fuss is about.

Only sticky moment came when I tried to look back. Supported body on one hand, swivelled torso round. Felt very wobbly. Swayed about and had to collapse on front to avoid falling.

(MEMO: Tracksuit not ideal garment for stair-climbing. Nor are socks – very slippery. Recommend wearing boots.)

Planned to get to top. Don't know why. Because it was there, I suppose.

Only about three steps from summit when arrested by scream from below. Recognised Her voice. Half-turned to see Her. Swayed dangerously.

Her face white. Paralysed with fear. Shrieked: 'Don't move! For God's sake, don't move!'

True to form, I ignored this and decided to show off my new climbing – or rather, abseiling – skills. I decided to reverse. Hadn't actually tried reverse, but when has lack of experience ever stopped me before . . . ?

Reverse much more difficult than forward.

Lowered one foot on to step below.

Lowered other foot.

Suddenly felt strong gravitational pull. Tried to grip at steps above with hands. No purchase. Felt ridges of steps thump against abdomen as I descended.

Abseiling without rope.

Caught by Her halfway down.

She sobbing, tears pouring down face. Hugged me to Her. Kept repeating, 'How did you do it? How did you get out?'

(NB: When hysterical She doesn't add 'then' to the end of questions.)

No chance of course that I'd give Her the answers She wanted. Just name and number.

Still, it was a good day's work. Mission accomplished, I'd say.

# DAY 24

She tried something different with me this morning. She was very busy, because for some reason She imagined She could get away with giving a nice civilised dinner party this evening (fond hopes – doomed to be dashed, of course). As a result, She wanted to spend the entire morning infiltrating garlic into more or less everything She could find in the kitchen.

And She wanted me out of the way.

She put me in my playpen (which has, since my famous break-out, been permanently mended and reinforced with maximum security rivets – the only way I could get out of it now is by tunnelling into the carpet), and She put down the traditional pile of plastic rattles, ducks, telephones, hammers, cars and other objects now too misshapen to be identified – for me to bang, chew and puke over.

Well, She ought to have realised by now that that little lot holds my attention for about 0.0000000001 of a second. I didn't even bother to pick any of them up, just got straight into the screaming.

She can never last for long when I really open up the

throttle. This time She managed to get her apron on and slice into one clove of garlic before the awful thought struck Her – THAT THERE MIGHT REALLY BE SOMETHING WRONG WITH ME.

(This, incidentally, is a useful tip in all dealings with parents. If they start thinking that you're just playing up and making a fuss about nothing, I recommend a sudden change in screaming. This involves going quiet for a few seconds and then letting out an almighty shriek, which never fails to bring the average parent hurtling to your side.)

And if they ever get blasé about the sudden change in screaming, there's nothing to beat the old self-inflicted injury.

Not as hard as it sounds. A satisfactory flesh-wound can easily be achieved by falling over, falling from a height or banging some part of your anatomy against something. Practice will teach you how to achieve maximum visual effect with the minimum of pain.

Though your self-inflicted injury shouldn't hurt at all, you still of course must scream like you're having all your fingernails pulled out.

Very few parents, when they finally give in and find you dripping blood, can help themselves from picking you up and saying, 'Oh, you poor little darling! You really *had* hurt yourself! Oh, what a naughty Mummy/Daddy I've been! I'll never forgive myself!'

Great thing is, they never do. Carry the guilt to their graves.

Anyway, getting back to my main drift, this morning She tried a new way of keeping me quiet. Switched on the television.

'There,' She cooed. 'There's a nice children's programme on. Lots of uvvy ickle animals and music and colour. Oo'll love this, won't oo then?'

Well, I gave it a chance. Looked at it for a full minute before coming to the conclusion that it was even more boring than the traditional pile of plastic rattles, ducks, telephones, hammers, cars and other objects now too misshapen to be identified.

If She imagines She's going to be able to keep me quiet by plonking me in front of the television all day, She's living in a fantasy world.

There are no soft options in dealing with me, and the sooner She comes to terms with that fact, the better.

# Twelfth Month

## DAY 2

Her mother arrived this morning with a present for me. 'It's an early Christmas or an early birthday present,' she announced.

I unwrapped it. My parents think this is a very clever trick, but there's nothing to it, as far as I'm concerned. I treat a present just the same as any other object that's handed to me – I grab hold of it and pull off any bits that will come off. With presents this tends to be the wrapping paper. Once I've removed that, I then see if any other bits come off.

Nothing else would come off the one I got this morning. It was a solid moulded plastic object. A potty.

She looked at it with some annoyance. 'It's too early. I've already told you – we'll get on to all that when we're ready for it and not before.'

'It's never too early,' Her mother countered. 'It's just a matter of discipline. Like weaning.'

'Don't bring weaning into this.'

'I'm sorry, but I have to say it, darling. If you'd stuck to your guns when you started weaning back in – '

'We're not talking about weaning. We're talking about a potty, Mother.'

'Very well, dear. All I want to say is that if a baby gets used to the idea of the potty being there early enough, then using it will come more naturally.'

'No, it won't,' said She.

'Yes, it will,' said Her mother. 'All of you children were out of nappies by fourteen months.'

'Yes, and look how neurotic we all turned out!' She snapped.

Like eating, toilet training is clearly going to be a perfect tool for emotional blackmail.


# DAY 12

Still haven't made a final decision on the first word business.

This morning, while She was dressing me, I very nearly let one slip out by mistake.

'Ooh,' She was saying. 'You are being such a little sod! You're being so . . . so . . . ooh, I don't know what the word is . . . '

I so nearly said 'Obstreperous.'

Probably just as well I didn't.

# DAY 17

A new excitement today – paper chains.

Apparently we're getting near Christmas and She's clearly going to make a very big deal of it. Don't know if She always does, or whether it's in my honour.

As She put the paper chains up, She kept saying, 'Doesn't oo love the uvvy paper chains then? Isn't they pretty then? Doesn't oo like them then?'

The answer is, yes I do like them. But, needless to say, not to look at.

As usual, my opportunity came when the phone rang. Minute She was out the door, I crawled across to grab the end of the paper chain She was putting up and systematically began to shred it.

I found an unexpected ally in my efforts. The cat came and joined in, ripping the chain into confetti. It's the first time we've done anything together, me and the cat. Maybe a friendly relationship can develop between us after all.

Maybe not, though. I, cannier than the cat, heard Her put the phone down and made sure that, by the time She was back in the room, I had crawled away to the other side and was looking disapprovingly at the poor creature. Caught red-pawed.

It got smacked fiercely and did its customary bolting-through-the-cat-flap.

It'll be quite a while before that friendly relationship develops.

## DAY 18

They do keep going on about this first word business. 'I'm really looking forward to hearing the baby speak,' I over-heard Her murmuring rather gooily to Him this evening.

'I'm not so sure,' was His jocular reply. 'Maybe we won't like what we hear.'

There's many a true word spoken in jest. But I wouldn't be that cruel. Would I?

Mind you, it is tempting.

'And wouldn't it be lovely,' She went on, 'if the first word came out on Christmas Day . . . '

Sometimes Her naive optimism is so touching. On the other hand, why not? I'm not basically vindictive, and if my pronouncing my first word on Christmas Day is going to give harmless pleasure, why should I deny it to them?

Suppose I could say, 'Happy Christmas!' That would certainly be seasonal and appropriate.

Or I could do the full Tiny Tim routine and say, 'God bless us, every one!' Though I think that might be a bit corny.

My thoughts were interrupted by Him saying, 'Yes, that would be great. On Christmas Day. When both our parents are here . . . '

I see. It's not just for them. They want to show me off.

# DAY 20

I know exactly what they're playing at with this first word business.

They know Christmas Day is going to be unbelievably sticky with both sets of relations gathered in one small house. Don't they ever learn? The ghastliness of the christening should have dinned into them that basic rule of family planning: KEEP RIVAL GRAND-PARENTS APART.

I suppose what they're hoping is that I, by delivering a first word or some other new trick, will provide a diversion to keep the heat off them.

Dream on, parents, dream on.


# DAY 24

Don't know what they think they were doing this evening.

There I was, happily drifting off to sleep, when in they blundered, reeling and giggling slightly (obviously been getting into the Christmas spirit early) and tied an empty stocking on to the end of my cot. Then, a bit later, in they came again and replaced it with a full one. What is this?

Now I'm quite willing to go along with the whole Father Christmas charade in a few years' time, if it makes them happy. I'll write letters to stuff up the chimney, I'll hang

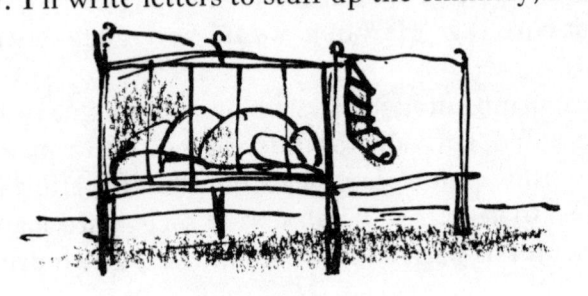

an empty stocking at the end of my bed, leave out a mince pie and a glass of whisky, and some crisps for the reindeer, and show amazement at the fact that my stocking has been filled by Christmas morning. But I'm not even one yet! Why on earth do they imagine that I will be able to appreciate the complex idea of a legendary benefactor who reputedly descends chimneys and philanthropically fills the stockings of well-behaved children?

Some things about my parents I will never understand.

## DAY 25

Christmas Day – as if I'd be allowed to forget it!

I woke up before they did and looked down to the end of my cot. Surprise, surprise – there was the stocking.

For a moment I considered falling on it and ripping out its contents. And then I thought – why make it easy for them? They can jolly well show me what to do with it.

My parents duly took me into their bed, and helped me to open my stocking. I dutifully ripped the paper off all the presents, while they cooed with delight as each one was revealed. There was something rather charming in the innocent glee on their faces.

'Oh, isn't that uvvy then?' they kept saying. 'Doesn't oo like Christmas then?'

I was tempted to use this moment for my first word. But I'm not sure that 'Humbug' would have gone down that well.

The morning dragged on with more Christmas jollity. I was decanted, specially for the occasion, into a smart new festive outfit, which, despite my most fervent efforts, they managed to keep free of splashes of soggy cardboard.

At noon His parents arrived, and were given drinks.

Five minutes later, Her parents arrived, and were given drinks.

They all raised their glasses.

'Well, this is jolly,' His parents said to Her parents. 'So good to see you.'

'Very good to see you too,' Her parents said to His parents. 'Pity it doesn't happen more often.'

'We must see to it that it does in the future,' His parents said to Her parents.

'Certainly must,' Her parents said to His parents.

A long silence descended. I contemplated breaking it with my first word: 'Hypocrites.'

Eventually we got on to Christmas lunch. That was pretty sticky too. In every sense.

Specially for the occasion, She'd puréed some turkey and Brussels sprouts for me, 'so that the baby can have what we're having.'

I'm afraid, after one mouthful, I had to reject it. She'd got the look and the consistency right, but that was all: it didn't *taste* right.

I was given a jar of Liver and Carrot. Now that *really* tasted like soggy cardboard.

After they had all bloated themselves, we sat by the tree to have more presents dished out.

Of the pile of loot round the bottom, at least half was for me. As I was handed each present, I pulled the paper off and pretended to be much more interested in that than the contents.

(I only did this because my parents kept saying that was what I always did, and my doing it seemed to amuse them.)

Her Christmas present to Him was a snooker cue. His to Her was some underwear which She was too shy to take out of the box in front of the massed parents.

To cover Her embarrassment, She turned to me. 'Now come on, shall we see what Granny and Grandad have got for oo then?' And She pushed a large package towards me.

I did my paper-ripping-off routine to reveal a big red push-along trolley full of bricks, which of course I ignored in favour of the torn paper.

I was aware of a bit of throat-clearing and then He said, 'Now come on, shall we see what Grandma and Grandpa have got for oo then?' And He pushed another large package towards me.

Need I tell you? I tore the wrapping paper off to reveal exactly the same trolley. It was even red.

There was lots of insincere laughing and assurances on both sides that they 'didn't mind at all', but it was clear they did. Deeply. The level of conviviality in the room dropped even further.

Don't know why they were getting so upset. It can't

have been rivalry for my interest, because as usual I was very even-handed and ignored both presents equally.

In the end, my day's haul was not bad. Apart from the two trolleys I am now the proud owner of three sort-and-post boxes, seven pull-along devices with noises (various), five bath toys (assorted), two xylophones and a whistle . . . to go alongside all the other sort-and-post boxes, pull-along devices, bath toys, etc., etc., that I already possess and never play with.

Meanwhile, the adults continued opening their presents. Each unwrapping was followed by insincere shrieks of 'Oh, just what I wanted!' and 'Thank you so much!', and every time I pulled the paper off one of mine, She would ask, 'What does oo say then? What does oo say then?'

But for that note of desperation in Her voice, I wouldn't have done it, but all this prompting showed how agonisingly much She needed me to come up with my first word as the only hope of saving the day.

So I relented. As I pulled the paper off yet another lump of plastic, She demanded frantically, 'What does oo say then?'

I could see Him across the room trying to pot a ball into a flowerpot with the present She had given him and I waved my arms excitedly towards Him, and said, quite distinctly: 'Cue.'

'Oh, listen!' She shrieked in excitement. 'That was baby's first word!'

'What did baby say? What did baby say?' He and the assembled relatives clamoured.

She smiled triumphantly. '"Thank you"!'

I corrected Her. 'Cue.'

'There!' she cried. 'Baby's said it again!'

I give up. If I'd wanted to say 'Thank you', that's what I would have said.

'God,' I asked silently while all around me raved in ecstasy about what a clever and polite baby I was, 'why couldn't I have been born to parents who had just a modicum of intelligence?'


# DAY 26

She has developed an infuriating new habit. Now, every time She gives me something, She says, 'And what do oo say then?'

I should have known this would happen. Well, I won't be doing it again. After the way they misunderstood me last time, I'm not going to use the word 'Cue' in a hurry!

# DAY 30

Hooray, hooray! Today I fulfilled a long-held desire.

Using my developing skills of movement and coordination, I actually managed to stand up in my cot and grab hold of THAT BLOODY MOBILE!

I clutched the bottom fluffy crocodile and put all my weight on it. The string broke immediately, and the whole lot came tumbling down on top of me.

I sucked and chewed at as many of the little beasts as I could, and I'm glad to say that they didn't turn out to be very robust.

Wonderful what you can do when you've got teeth. I don't think there's any danger of them trying to re-assemble the sodden mass of shredded fabric and bent plastic that they retrieved from the bottom of my cot.

# DAY 31

The end of my first year, and an appropriate time for an assessment of progress over the last twelve months.

Well, overall not too bad. It hasn't always been easy. There have been inevitable setbacks, some lessons learnt more slowly than others, some basic skills yet to be acquired.

And there have of course been behavioural problems – temper tantrums when things didn't go absolutely right first time, some peevish reactions to the inevitable disciplines of any situation in which people have to live together, a tardiness in developing social poise and rather too much evidence of plain, old-fashioned selfishness.

Nor has there been as much progress on the weaning front as some authorities might have wished for.

But let's be charitable, in keeping with the spirit of the approaching New Year. Let's forget all the difficulties, squabbles and unseemly power contests. Let's concentrate on the positive achievements of the last twelve months.

No, generally speaking, my parents aren't shaping up too badly.